A Loss Mum's Journal...

A Memoir: Life after losing you

by

Danielle Benedict

Cover design by Scott Gaunt: scottgaunt@hotmail.co.uk

Photographs by © Remember My Baby. Used with permission.

Feather illustration from Freepik.com.

Quotes by F. Scott Fitzgerald from *The Beautiful and Damned* and *Flappers and Philosophers.*

Quote by Lewis Carroll, from *Alice in Wonderland.*

Quote by Virginia Woolf from *Night and Day.*

Quote by A. A. Milne from *The Complete Tales of Winnie-the-Pooh.*

Immortality (Do Not Stand By My Grave and Weep) by Clare Harner.

I dedicate this to all the loss mums out there and to every special angel baby. But most importantly, I wrote this book for you little miss, and for me. My love for you grows every day and I hope that I am making you proud. Always and forever, I love you.

Olivia-Grace 26/02/2019 – 04/04/2019

Author's Note

This book is a memoir. It reflects the authors recollection of personal experiences and emotions and is true to their memory. Some events have been compressed, and some dialogue may have been recreated slightly. All characters are real individuals, and those who are named give their permission. The author has been inspired in their writing from online support groups, grief quotes and images, and from fellow loss mums.

A content warning for readers, this book discusses infant loss and includes photos which some may find upsetting.

Every effort has been made to attribute correctly and get permission from copyright holders.

Acknowledgements

I appreciate everyone who has been and continues to be supportive of me in this journey. To those who have surfed the grief waves alongside me, pulling me up for air when I was drowning, and the kind and gentle faces who I will never forget in those painful moments. Olivia-Grace, you have left imprints on many hearts.

A special thank you and recognition to the UK registered charity, ©Remember My Baby, for capturing some beautiful memories.

And a gracious and forever thank you to the man who co-created the most precious and wanted baby.

"How lucky am I to have something that makes saying goodbye so hard."

A.A. Milne,

The Complete Tales of Winnie-the-Pooh

Preface...

I have experienced the worst tragedy and injustice of my life. I say that with confidence, because I simply cannot imagine anything more horrific than the reality that is my life right now. I have lost my baby. I have experienced pain, love, and anger so raw that I see the broken pieces of my mind, heart, and soul looking back at me in the mirror. I have experienced the intense isolation of feeling completely alone, even when surrounded by familiar faces. And because I have experienced this, I know that there are other women out there, somewhere, who are sobbing quietly into their pillows, their tears flowing like a river down the shower drain, smelling the beautiful scent of their child's clothes, still soft to touch, and smelling so deeply of them. An ongoing battle so fierce, you don't know how you will ever recover and come out alive. But let me tell you this, Mama: you will survive. Not as the same person, but you will survive and live again. You will breathe again. You will laugh again. You are new. You have known a love so primitive, so passionate, so relentless that you have no option but to survive this, Mama. You will survive, for your angel baby.

I have been writing to you, my little miss, my sweet angel baby, because it doesn't matter how many minutes you blessed my world with, your memory will last beyond a lifetime. I promised to tell our story, and the journey of our first year living with the grief of losing you. And I need other mothers to know they are not alone. That somehow, we will hold each other, carry each other, drag each other along if we have to, if our hearts and feet are just too heavy on the ground. I need you to know, Olivia-Grace, that you are not alone. Your precious baby body may have left this world, but you are most certainly still living on. You are living on in so many hearts, and I know you are always with me.

OLIVIA-GRACE
It should have been me...

*T*here was a day, not too long ago, when I thought I was going to die. The adrenaline was wearing off, and the overwhelming tones, beeps and alarms of the daytime madness was simply a memory of yesterday's shift. At 3 a.m. when the quiet and darkness of the NICU lit up my life like an explosion of fireworks, and I looked at your tiny body, foreign with wires and pads, I fell to the floor, sure I was about to die.

But I didn't die.
You did.
My first baby...

Hypoxic Ischemic Encephalopathy. HIE. No, I had never heard of it before either. For you, a death sentence caused by a starvation of oxygen during labour, damaging your brain beyond repair. A tongue-twister of an injury that I would compulsively research and google when my tired eyes allowed it. Five weeks of intense reading and trying to understand what the hell had happened to my perfect baby girl and her already incredible brain. An injury as complex in nature and consequences as it is difficult to say. I will never forget the look on the doctor's face, soon after you were born: *Brain damage, brain damage...* That was all I could hear, through her worried, strained expression. *Do you understand me, Dani? ... Brain damage, brain damage...* Every other word slurred together as though she were talking to me in a foreign language. *Brain damage, brain damage...*

Well, that's what happened to you, my little miss. And we still don't know why. They don't know why. Maybe you do? Maybe I will never know and maybe that's okay? I suppose to know why you were taken from me would only magnify the pain you left behind. Because at least this way, I can only try to keep the faith that in some bizarre and unfair twist of fate, this was all meant to happen. That from the minute you were made, your life purpose was to be my angel, forever watching over me. In desperate moments, I find just a little bit of peace believing that.

A beautiful baby girl, and your name is Olivia-Grace. You blessed me with a perfect pregnancy, but at 36 weeks you knew something was wrong, and you had to get out.

The memory of the delivery is just a jumbled mess in my foggy brain, coated in fear and terror. A room full of strange faces looking at me, waiting patiently for me to give that last push and you would be outside the "safety" of my womb. Safety; what a load of shit. It turns out you weren't safe, and now neither am I. But in that moment, just before you were born, all I felt was fear. Our bond strengthened then, because I believe that we both instinctively knew something was wrong. The delivery, now, is simply a nightmare incident that will haunt me for the rest of my life. Birth trauma is not something they warn you about at your routine midwife appointments, and my innocent brain had no idea this was even a thing. You came into this world so quickly, I didn't even acknowledge that my life had changed in every way possible until I looked so hard at you much later in the day, that my eyes hurt. I was in a state of shock and numb from the catastrophic events of the day, not understanding anything that was going on, but snuggled inside a medical incubator my eyes found something precious to fixate on. The first thing I properly noticed were your perfectly formed, sweetest feet. Ten absolutely stunning toes, and long, long feet. You get those feet from your mama. That was the only part of you I was able to hold, the day you were born. My hands were shaking with nerves and anticipation as I ran my fingers over your baby soft skin, finally touching what had been kicking my ribs so passionately over the past few months. A new obsession in my life began that day. I would kiss your feet multiple times a day, from that day forward.

Although I was the one to live, holding you as you put on your angel wings five weeks later, a part of me died alongside you. I don't know if that part was a piece of my heart, a piece of my soul, my world? Perhaps a combination of all three. All I know is that for a brief time in my life, I felt complete. An inexplicable sense of wholeness. The day you closed your eyes for the last time took away that sense of peace. Only to be replaced with a cold and constant state of emptiness. On that day I became a "loss mum". That void can never be filled. I wouldn't even attempt to try. Because the piece of "me" that went up to heaven with you that day can never be resuscitated. Although, as the days go on, and I find things to distract myself with, and positive things to accomplish, in every other moment and in every other thought, there you are. My little miss that I was so fortunate to meet, to hold, to kiss. I can still smell you, a scent of perfection lingering in the air around me. I'm told that the days get easier. I'm told that time will help to heal a wound so deep it cannot be seen. But the truth is, my little miss... I will never heal. Not completely. Because with every tear, every "what if", every memory, I'm reminded that I am no longer the same person. That you, my perfect baby girl, are no longer with me. And I made a promise to you that I would keep moving forward, that I would bravely and proudly tell your story as I stood in front of grief, wounded and weak but not missing courage, wondering, can grief be both my enemy and my friend? That promise I will honour. You will be my shield, protecting those wounds that can never, truly, be healed.

A letter from your grandma...

Olivia-Grace; To the moon and back...

The day you came into our lives, 26 February 2019. A day that should have been filled with joy was the day our worlds came crashing down around us, and pain unlike anything I have ever felt before became a new and constant part of my life.

The day started early, with me waking up to find your mummy in a lot of pain, and so after a call to the maternity unit we headed off to the hospital. I was certain she was in labour, and I was a little nervous but excited too. I was finally going to meet my first grandchild. When we got to the maternity ward it was confirmed your mum was in labour and as she had progressed quite a lot, we were taken straight to the delivery ward. It was go time. From there things just moved at breakneck speed, so quick that there was no time to process what was happening. Nor was there any time to give your mum any pain relief. Your mum was working hard, and I felt so helpless, but she was supported by a doctor, and while I was anxious seeing my baby in so much pain and with the labour moving so quickly, I had no reason to think that there was anything to be worried about.

Then, our world stopped and came crashing down on us.

Suddenly the small room was full of people. The midwives were encouraging your mum to push but she was getting so tired and was in so much pain. She was doing the best she could, but I know to this day she blames herself for not being able to get you out quickly enough. A guilt she should not have to carry, yet she does. The room, despite the urgency and rush of you wanting to come, was calm. Looking back now, that calmness fuels the anger. How could they all have been so calm?

Calm... Until you were born.

I watched you come into the world and my heart simply broke. You were passed to the paediatric team immediately who started to help you. Numb is the only way to describe how I felt. Numb and helpless. We all seemed to be waiting and holding our breath. I remember your mum asking why you weren't crying, but I can't remember if anybody answered her. I can only remember silence.

We waited, and waited – in silence; there were no words. Your mum sat at the window and I stood. And at last, a doctor came to speak to her and the news was not good.

Your mum and I went to see you before saying goodbye for you to be transferred to a specialist unit. There wasn't much of you that we could see as you were covered in a cooling blanket, wires and eye protection, but lying so delicately at the bottom of the incubator were your feet. Your beautiful feet that we were able to touch.

They had given you a special teddy for the journey, and then you were gone.

Most of the time in the NICU was spent at your crib side. Praying that you would be okay. You had your own nurse to look after you and although you were small you were not the smallest baby in the unit. It seemed so backwards, that the biggest of the bunch, most perfectly formed, would be fighting the hardest of battles. You looked so healthy from the outside.

During our stay in the hospital, we learnt how to care for you, which was scary. We read books to you, sang, and talked to you, changed your nappy and your mum gave you your milk. Your mum was so strong. I was always proud of my girl but during this time she took my breath away. She was a big support to me and the other parents we met, and I think it helped her to help others.

The day came when I was asked if I wanted to hold you; of course I did but I was scared as well. You were still on the ventilator, so the nurses put up a screen and two of them settled you in my arms and secured all your tubes to me so that they didn't move. I was so terrified that I would do something to hurt you, and while it felt so good to have you close to me, my heart broke all over again.

I had not wanted to cry in front of your mum but once the nurses left and I was on my own behind the screen, I could not hold my tears back and cried as quietly as I could. You were perfect, our own little wonder woman. It was so unfair that you were so ill and that your mum was in so much pain. I was so angry but didn't want to show it. I don't know how much help I was to your mum, but I wouldn't have wanted to have been anywhere else but with her, and you. My baby, and my grandbaby.

For five weeks your mum and I lived on a rollercoaster of highs and lows. I don't like to remember the low times, it hurts, but I do remember the joy we felt the first time we saw your eyes. You made us wait, but my strong baby girl would finally open her eyes. We had been praying for that. You had the most beautiful eyes.

The rest... well, I'm still trying to navigate this new life of grief and love. But I do know that while we only had you for a short time, we made the most of every moment we could, and although my heart still breaks from missing you, there are memories that we made that I will cherish for the rest of my life.

Love you to the moon and back, my little angel. Till we meet again, Grandma XOXO

Olivia-Grace, 10 of the sweetest toes that fit so perfectly
in the palm of my hand

A decision I shouldn't make...

It was a Wednesday, around lunch time. We had been called back into "that room" for another "chat". By now I knew exactly what these "chats" entailed, and they never got any easier. Every week the room seemed to get darker, and smaller, and more suffocating. Your brain damage was severe, and global. There are only so many times someone should have to hear the words "brain damage". Irreparable. Terminal. Cerebral palsy. And I was so, so tired of hearing it. Couldn't they see how tired I was? They kept telling me what you would never do. Everything that you simply couldn't do. Is that all they saw when they looked at you? Didn't it matter what I saw? I saw something precious. And to me you were perfect. But on this particular Wednesday, the consultant neonatologist needed to tell me that we were out of options, out of resources, out of luck. And I had to make a decision. The damage to your brain was so deep, it had affected your most primal reflexes. I just couldn't fathom that your body, neck down, was just perfect and healthy. But your brain was so broken it had caused you to suffer bilateral vocal cord palsy, and I knew what this meant. Without the breathing tube you would not live. With the breathing tube, what life would I force you to live? You would never have the life you should have had. You would never have the life I had dreamt for you. And when my brain accidentally goes back to that day, sitting in "that room", I break out in the same angry, blazing red patch of hives, my body trembles and my throat feels as though it is going to close. PTSD is a bitch.

I already knew what my decision would be, though I was so scared to say it out loud. I can't risk you thinking this was an easy choice for me. There was nothing easy about committing to do the hardest thing I'll ever have to do. But how could I possibly ask more of you when you had already shown a lifetime's worth of bravery and determination? I don't regret the decision I made, and I try not to think about being the one to sign that clinical, morbid form, because that is just an unbearable load for a mother to burden. DNAR. End of life care. *Sign here Danielle*, a pen nudged into my clammy and shaking hands, *sign here please*, inked with torture and a broken heart. It caused me utter agony, but it was so that I could spare you another day of physical pain, so it must have been the right call, right? I don't think anyone could ever be truly at peace knowing they'd had to be the one to consent to removing the one thing keeping you with me.

You know, people always ask me about your birth. When, how long, did I get pain relief? They are curious whether you came out the southern route, or whether I was cut open to set you free. *What exactly went wrong, Dani?* Why do they want to know? Talk of your actual death makes them uncomfortable, but I guess there is a subconscious feeling of hope, excitement and potential surrounding the talk of birth that they are still interested in, even though they know the outcome. I don't mind telling them about how you came into this world. Maybe talking about it helps with my grief journey. But I do wish they would also ask about your death. I want them to know that you were held, and loved so hard, right until the end. That you didn't suffer or feel any kind of pain. That you lay in our arms dressed so perfectly and neatly in your mummy and me sleeper, like a doll, smothered in love. I think I need them to know that, so they won't associate you with what we normally think death is like. Dark, despairing, and if you're lucky, it comes when you're old, surrounded by family and a lifetime's worth of memories. Death and babies are two words that should not be in the same sentence. We grow up learning about death and dying. We come to realise and accept that it's a sad reality that one day we will have to say goodbye to our grandparents, our own parents, maybe friends and siblings. But we never grow up thinking that the death of our child will come before us. Maybe this is why this type of grief is so complex and confusing. It's just all so wrong, and backwards. It just doesn't make sense that I would know the date of your death before it even happened. Planning for my baby's death…how fucked up, I will never wrap my brain around that. And so, when the time came and everything was prepared for us, we would have a sleepover in the hospice and I would hold you so tight and coat you in all my love, because that is what you deserved. Cuddling your Dumbo teddy bear, and free from all of the awful wires and tubes, you would die in the arms of your mummy and daddy.

A letter from Aunty Briony...

Olivia-Grace: Let me tell you a funny story...

Olivia-Grace, your mummy had sent me out on a shopping mission before coming to lay my eyes on you for the very first time.

She had asked me to pick up breast pads. Breast pads!!? I am not the obvious choice of shopper for such things.

Well, I walked round and round the store, up and down the aisles of baby bits, and could I find them? No!

In the end I asked a young shop assistant to help me. It turns out I wasn't looking for anything that resembled shoulder pads from the 1980s! Then, when she asked me, "Would you like small, medium or large?" I proceeded to cup my own breasts and say to the young girl, "Well, she's not as big as me!" Imagine my horror when she blushed, shying away from my gesturing hands, and advised me that she had in fact meant box size!

I'm so very sorry I will never get the chance to tell you that story in person. But I know that a beautiful pair of angel ears will be listening in when your mummy and I have a giggle, reminiscing over that story. Aunty B, and the hunt for breast pads!

Very much love my darling, Aunty Briony

Goodbye is a shit word...

You would think that the hardest day of our lives would be the day you went to sleep for eternity, but at least I have the memory of kissing you one last time. I have never felt more terror in my life than when I looked at the front door to the hospice, knowing what was waiting for us on the other side. Pain, death and shattered, broken hearts. I was terrified, and all morning I had random attacks of anxiety and panic, that made me want to just run away and not face any of this. I wanted my own mum to carry me and make me feel safe, the way she did when I was a child. But now I was a mother myself, and I knew I had to do the same for you. You left my body to come into this world, and so you would leave, cradled tightly in my arms. I crept, tiny steps, closer and closer to that door. That door. The door I am so afraid of.

As much as I want to, and I try, I will never be able to forget that day; the sounds, the cold breeze running through the ancient house they remodelled into a hospice, the feel of the unknown bed as we lay as a family of three for the first, and last, time. Such a sad sense of everything wrong with the world, lingering stagnant in the air. A children's hospice. So many broken hearts and missing faces in family photos. It's the beginning of feeling your absence in everything I do, and I don't dare breathe it in. Before going to the bedroom where your passing would take place, we had a priest come, and we gathered in the hospice lounge. I am not particularly religious, although over the past weeks, while trying to live through this storm, I have found myself questioning so many things. I've been looking for God, asking fate what twisted game we are playing, desperate to know is there anybody out there that can tell me what went so wrong? I have been searching for answers and guidance, because none of this has made any sense. But your grandmother, your *Abuela,* is very religious. She is a committed and loyal Catholic and this was important to her, and she was important to me. Her faith is so strong and I knew her heart was torn apart, that if having you baptised before leaving this Earth brought her some comfort in this tragic time, I would accommodate that blessing. But I didn't need to have you officially baptised to know you were going somewhere magical. I believed after you took your last breath there would be an angel waiting for you, likely my own nana, and you would be taken somewhere safe to heal. I had privately whispered to my nana on the

20

muted drive to the hospice, asking her to come and stay closely by our sides and to be there waiting for you, to greet you with love and guide you to where you needed to go. My nana was so special to me; a wonderfully kind, clever and spiritual woman, and I needed to believe you wouldn't be alone, lost in a new world. Looking back now though, I am so grateful that we found a compassionate priest to come and bless you, and dampen your tiny forehead with holy water. Not because I think that it was necessary for you to go to Heaven, but because my own heart found a small amount of peace and reassurance, watching him and your grandmother speak beautiful prayers whilst holding their symbolic gold cross that dangled from their necks. The dedication to their faith that no matter this pain, we will all be taken care of and somehow live through this. That no God out there would let you suffer as your soul slipped away, leaving the body that was broken behind. Before going to "that room", I let myself embrace and believe it all, and allowed the strength of their faith to take care of me and what was about to come.

I hated the purple in that bedroom and the uncomforting pictures on the wall. It wasn't your room, or ours, but I suppose a room that felt so "wrong" was the right fit for the scene that never should have happened. I will always look back at that day with regret though, baby. That is where we would lie as they removed your breathing tube, and you would eventually, after taking small gasps for air, each one feeling like my own heart would stop, pass away. I was completely selfish by the very end. I was entirely broken down to my core, empty and burnt. As you took your last breath, and I had one final kiss, and I laid your body back down on the bed, I ran. At the time all I could think about was getting to the safety of my home and hiding in the familiar comfort of my own bed. Everything that had happened to us those past five weeks had been so unknown, so alien and terrifying, I just needed something that I knew, if that makes sense. I couldn't wait any longer to throw my body under the warmth of my duvet and close the curtains on the world, and somehow, I'd plan to stay there until I died, or what seemed the less likely option; until I could face a life that didn't seem so cruel and painful anymore. At the start, I really did think I would stay in bed forever. And at the very end, the goal of just making it to my own resting place was all I could think about.

I'll always regret now not holding you for longer, not breathing you in harder, letting your head rest in the nook of my neck. You fit me so perfectly; all along you had been my missing piece. I regret not staying to help your daddy give you one last bath and get you dressed. Your perfectly tiny body on the bed, washed and clean and, for the first time in over five weeks, completely naked; so innocent, so loved, so still. My hands were shaking so hard I didn't dare try to touch or lift you. The weight of your tiny body was just too heavy for me. I hate myself for running, but please understand, baby girl, leaving you behind was the most torturous thing a mama can do, and if I had stayed and got lost in a world of just you and me, I don't think I could have ever left. Please forgive me, and maybe one day I will forgive myself.

The day you went to sleep blurs in my head now. I try not to go there too much; it hurts and mostly I don't feel strong enough. But it's there for when I do choose to remember; it will always be there. But when I think about the day I found the hardest, it was the day of the funeral; that takes first place. The day of the funeral took over my body with such force, I wasn't sure I was even going to see it through. I suppose an element of "survival" had worn off, and now I was simply weak. *Where the hell am I going to find that level of courage, to watch my daughter's body be taken away, only to be set alight and brought home not in a swaddle blanket as you should, but in a box? Hadn't I already been through enough?*

Up until this day I could try to imagine you were just fast asleep, in another bedroom, dreaming of all the magical things one could dream of. I could imagine you safe, and comfortable, and happy. But the day I had to sit next to you in a clinical, white box felt like a knife straight through my heart. Because I knew that this was really it. It wasn't some horrific nightmare that I might wake up from. That despite all the praying, and wishing, and bargaining one could do, there was no miracle to be had, for me, nor for you.

I was incredibly proud of your daddy in that moment. When he walked his daughter down the aisle. There isn't a word to describe how wrong that moment was for him, but he stood so tall and held you firmly yet gently in his arms. He was giving you one final cuddle as he carried the smallest, yet heaviest, of coffins. We had requested that we go in first, an empty chapel echoing silence as we crept baby steps, with our baby. I was so afraid I would simply collapse in front of a room full of people. And I had wanted a private moment as we rested you on the much too large table, at the front for all to see. I had needed that moment to ask you once again, to give me strength, and to tell you just how much I loved you. But once we reached our seats and our beloved friends and family began to enter, I turned around seeking out my best forever people, still wearing my sunglasses to hide my dagger like tears, and the biggest hug and simple words... *we've got you...* found their way to me.

I had asked that no one wear black. Yellow or pink, those were your colours. And daffodils. I wanted to see a room filled with daffodils and splashes of sweet baby pink. Daffodils will forever be my favourite flower now. When the NICU was home for both of us, every early morning, as the sun was just rising, I would walk from the residential flats over to the main hospital, still half asleep and sore, carrying the bottles of milk I had pumped for you in the middle of the night. And each morning I passed a beautiful green patch of grass with a vibrant centrepiece of budding daffodils. They flowered early your year. Every morning I would walk past those daffs and their beauty, and I would feel hope. A spring flower signifying a new season was coming; the darkest and longest days of winter were over. A brighter time was almost here. And I couldn't help feeling hopeful. That was how I wanted to start every day with you, baby girl, hopeful. And now, I am in love with those yellow bursts of spring and everything they mean to me.

The room was full, and everyone had followed my wish. Not a black item in sight. Just vibrant, pretty colours, for a pretty little girl. Your wonderful aunty Briony had been busy making delicate friendship bracelets in your colours. A bracelet for each and every one of us to wear on that day. A symbol of support and love, worn proudly to unite us all and acknowledge just how important you are. That bracelet is still on my wrist, little miss, and I don't plan on taking it off. The celebrant, an older man named John, a name I will surely never forget, had a face made up of sparkling eyes that loved to laugh, and a kind smile, and he did us so proud. He conducted your ceremony with dignity and class. It didn't matter that you were a little person; he showed you all the respect and love you deserved, and offered his own daffodil pin to you as a symbol of admiration and tribute. I remember him telling us afterwards that your service was actually his first for a baby. And how in awe he was, seeing the chapel so full. I don't think he will ever forget you, little miss. Another person you have imprinted on. Small comforts when I look back to my darkest day are so important, I think.

Remembering those details helps me block out the trauma of walking down the aisle, my whole weight against my mum, because my legs just couldn't stand. The music. I had chosen such a graceful song for you, but the soft melody and calming tones did nothing to ease my nerves or steady my heart. But somehow, we made it through. The memory of the day now is very hazy, hours blended, emotions blurred. After the ceremony we held a wake for you at a local hotel. A beautiful building, with beautiful gardens, and we were very lucky that on such an awful day, the weather was so nice. Food, drink, every table had an engraved vase filled with daffodils, and your photo. Your face for all to see, at every turn. Your funeral flowers were displayed at the entrance, the sweet and gentle bouquet of baby breath, and a single daffodil arranged into a heart. I wish I had had the forethought to do something special with your flowers after that day. Preserve them in some way so they could never die. I've seen such wonderfully creative things since then; pressed flowers in resin, tributes and memorials of tokens from the funeral, that not keeping your flowers will forever be a regret.

I always wondered what the staff thought as they were setting up our room, ready to host a crowd of broken hearts. They never asked who the wake was for when we booked, and I was too afraid to bring you up in the conversation.

Did they now look at me with pity and sadness? Did they think you were the prettiest baby they had ever seen? Did they agree that life sometimes is just completely and utterly miserable and unfair? I floated about that room on autopilot. I usually love to host, and so it was easy for me to mingle and chat, thank everyone for their kind words and sympathies, all the while never really being there. I don't know where I was, but I wasn't in that room. My brain was back in survival mode, and there was a protective bubble around my fragile body; I had been carried off to somewhere safe. I could feel my lungs expanding, my lips moving and creating sound, but inside, I was dead. By the end of the evening, still with a glass of white wine in hand and a beaten heart, very close friends and family remained. We sat snugly around the table, sharing our tears. We talked about you, we remembered you and we made a promise. We were so grateful for you, and I still felt blessed, even at the funeral of my daughter, because you had chosen me. It was a very intimate, surreal time. You brought us all so close together that day. An indescribable bond of strength and love, and a reminder that we will always be there for each other.

Why are funerals so final? I'd already dedicated my life to remembering you. To doing wonderful things in your name for others. So why did this day matter so much? I know why. It was the last time your amazing little body would be whole on this Earth. The last time you would leave a recognized footprint behind. It's the last time that something so precious on this planet belonged to me, and only me. With your body burnt, still hugging your Dumbo teddy I'd loved so much, you truly and irretrievably were gone.

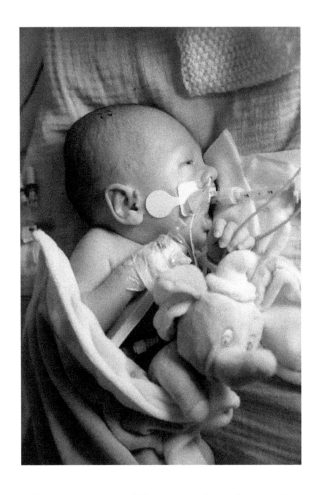

Olivia-Grace, cuddling your Dumbo comforter

OLIVIA-GRACE
A gift from Heaven...

I had accepted my reality that, after you died, I would spend countless days in bed. Crying uncontrollably, lost in a swirling, chaotic pit of darkness. And while the world as I had known it had been shaken to its very core, I did get out of bed – on day three, I think it was. Days sooner than anyone had expected of me, that I had even expected of myself. I lay in bed, suffocating on the stale air around me. A pit of denial and sadness. So many thoughts racing through my mind. It was so tiring, so I tried to find one "good" thought. A positive one, and that would be the drive I needed to put on some clothes and walk down my very normal staircase, sit at my normal breakfast table and have a very normal cup of extra strong coffee. All the while, these things around me that were so normal reminded me that I was far from it.

I felt so different, soul deep. It was like I was walking in someone else's body, watching this frail and beaten girl try to navigate how to put one foot in front of the other. A baby myself, falling, rolling, learning. Has the shock and intensity of grief forced me to revert back to a childlike state of vulnerability? Is it normal to feel this way?

I have lost my sense of identity, meaning and purpose in the blink of an eye, and that is just so terrifying. The thief that is death has robbed me in every way imaginable, and I don't know who I am anymore. But I kept this thought in my head, because I had promised you. Living requires us to move, and eat, and breathe. I don't have to enjoy it right now; I just have to do it. It all seemed so overwhelming, but just one thing at a time, I said to myself. *Just put on some clean pants, Dani, you stink.* While I lay in my messy bed of tangled sheets and the salty smell of sweat and tears, I thought endless things. I need to keep living, but how do I do that?

Questioning myself; I'm just a person. A regular person, with no idea of how to deal with this, or make the extraordinary changes I want to make. How do I stop other babies dying? How do I protect their brains, and their mothers' hearts? You. For the past five weeks my whole world has been centred around you, and what I can do to help. I don't want that to stop just because you are no longer lying just a few metres away from me. I can still feel you, so I will do something for you.

And so, when I got out of bed and dragged my weary body, sensitive to the daylight, downstairs to make a cup of wake-me-up juice, I sent out a group message. That message went to my favourite people on this planet: your aunties. I had to focus on this one good thought, fixate and obsess on it, to do something good in your name. In your memory. And so, I asked our ladies to start collecting toiletries, and pads, and everything "post birth" you could think of. I had no idea the lengths these women would go to, simply because of their love for you. Last weekend, a group of nine of us, Grandma and Daddy included, gathered around the kitchen table. The room was a steady hum of Disney songs, unexpected laughter and silly questions about breast pads and lactating. We were compiling care packages for the mamas on the NICU. The same NICU that we had inhabited for just over five weeks.

I organised it like a military operation. Stations dedicated to oral care, then body lotions and soap, so on and so on. For once, my compulsive disorder and need for control synched in perfect harmony with my loyal little worker bees. We made 88 care packages that night, all to be given to the mamas going through their own challenging and exhausting journey in the NICU. I felt so strongly that what we were doing would help someone else, and that in turn helped me. When the drama of the delivery was over, and you were rushed off to the intensive care unit, we raced so quickly behind you that the thought of anything necessary such as clothes and unbloodied pants for myself didn't even cross our minds. I had already packed a few things, but the excitement of getting ready and preparing a hospital bag for you to come was yet another thing that was taken away from me when you decided to come early. I think even then I was in such denial about what was really happening, and how long we could potentially be in the NICU, that my needs were at the very bottom of my priorities. All I knew was that we would not be coming home that night. No welcome home outfit. No car seat. No baby. I had no nappies for such a little bum. No breast pads for my keen and eager breasts, desperate to feed you. And an embarrassingly small pack of maternity pads, courtesy of my inexperience and naivety on how the body actually reacts to birth, to cushion the exit wound that would gush and scare the shit out of me. I knew nothing of life and body post birth, and I knew nothing of life on a NICU.

It broke my heart to think of other ladies, who in the haste of a premature delivery, or birth gone wrong, would also lie in the bed on the ward, wondering how they could stock up on essentials without the added humiliation of bleeding along the corridor floor in search of pads, or leaking milk onto their only clean(ish) pair of pyjamas. The last thing you want to do when your baby lies so helplessly is leave them there to go to the local supermarket. That was my drive when making these care packages. *I want to help you, Mama, so you can stay close, and help your baby.*

The following week, Daddy and I took the drive an hour away to the hospital that worked so hard to save you. I didn't feel too nervous. Not until I got to the front doors of the ward and the stench of "hospital" hit me in the face. Cue the stress hives creeping up my neck. Sweat balling up in the palms of my clenched fists. And silent tears that dared not leave the sunken bed of my eyes, only escaping as I finally remembered how to breathe. My body has not forgotten, and it reacted before my mind could even catch up. It seems so much longer ago now that I was walking these corridors in my sweatpants, no make-up and greasy hair. One thing on my mind only; to be next to you. It's amazing how you learn to adapt. You can learn to live anywhere, and for those five weeks, that place became our home. We were on a first-name basis with every member of staff, and I knew other parents from our unsocial meetings in the coffee room at 3 a.m. I was bare and stripped down to next to nothing. Just my body and a cold cup of tea and half eaten biscuit that sat next to me for three hours at a time. I was quickly humbled, and realised that material and superficial belongings no longer matter, because the only thing that is important in your life is lying in a hospital cot, needing you, with no care for what you're wearing or how you look. Your baby knows your voice and your smell, and suddenly, being next to your tiny, helpless child is the only thing in your life that will ever matter.

On that Wednesday, we arrived at the NICU armed with five large boxes filled to the brim with goody bags. And the look of appreciation and awe on the faces of our favourite nurses, who had arranged to meet us, was a gift in return for me. Three of them to be precise. And one doctor. Their names are Jess, Lynn, Sarah and, of course, the red-haired, smiley doctor, Florence. I really admired these women. I found hope in them. Their compassion, intelligence and grace helped me get through the NICU days more than they will ever know. I trusted them; I trusted them with your life. Not for one minute did I ever feel as though they were giving up on you. You can't see brain damage, and from the outside you were just so perfect, but even though they knew how poorly you were, they still refused to give up.

I hope you always had the sense that they were very much in love with you too, little miss. I know first-hand that sometimes there are certain patients who will stay with you forever. Maybe that is why I connected so purely with these women. Maybe that's why, for so many weeks, I had this sense of hope, because they worked so tirelessly to do all that they could for you. I face trauma, pain, and loss, on a daily basis at work, but it's someone else's story. If I'm honest, it always made me feel that if I dealt with other people's misfortune, I would never have to deal with something so horrendous myself. I was supposed to be the one saving others; someone wasn't meant to have to save me, or you. That Tuesday morning when you were born, the universe proved me wrong. My story had suddenly become somebody else's debrief. You, and our family, are one of those cases that pin directly onto someone's heart. The heart of a stranger. They all cried when you went away. I believe every day they prayed, and wished, and hoped as hard as we did for you to live. We brought each of them a beautifully smelly pink candle. That candle, every time it flickers in the dark, is you. And they will never forget you. The biggest, most beautiful baby on the ward. My baby.

And so, on that day, I believe that your gift from Heaven, a care package to ease the life of a scared and tired new mama, will bring a smile or two. And so already you have changed somebody's life. Somebody I will never even know. A large basket of pink and purple tote bags, with a sign above reading:

Life on the NICU is rough, remember to take care of yourself, Mama. In loving memory of my little miss. Olivia-Grace 26/02/19 – 04/04/19.

A letter from grandpa...

Olivia-Grace: A selfless love...

Much like the sun that rises every day to brighten the Earth, never asking for anything in return, my love for you knows no limits or favours. Look what happens with a love like that, so selfless and unconditional; it lights the whole sky. And so do you, my beautiful Olivia-Grace. You light up our sky, you light up our lives, even after the sun takes rest and sets for the day.

Sleep tight, little girl.

Love, from your grandpa xxx

OLIVIA-GRACE
Too many dates...

*I*t's so unfair, isn't it? That us loss mums have not only the special day you were born etched onto our hearts and brains, but also the day you left. The day, the time, the place. There is no need for a calendar, or reminder set, for us to recall these important dates. So many of them. Due dates, birthdays, death days, funeral days, Mother's Day, Mother's Day for the bereaved, a day to remember the babies who no longer walk this world with us; it seems the list goes on and on. Multiple dates, each bringing different and conflicting emotions and thoughts that, no matter what, will always centre around you. Today is your one-month anniversary, or as I have now come to call it, your Angel-versary. One month ago today we held you so close, tears cascading onto your beautiful head, like a waterfall, as I refused to take my lips off you. Simply saying, "We love you, baby girl. It's okay, we're here. You can go." I didn't know what else to say to you. Now, those words find their way into my ears when I'm sitting in silence, and I'm so startled I stop breathing... *It's okay. You can go.* I talked to you about our future adventures. About what we would do in the coming months, making sure to take your comforter with us at all times, so you could be a part of the journey. About your loyal protector and big sister of the fur kind, Naki. My beloved dog, who has saved me on more than one occasion, and once reunited at home, sensing my constant state of depression and anguish, would save me again. And I told you a promise. A promise, that as much as I wanted to go with you, I would live. I would live, even when I didn't want to. I promised you this. I chatted to you, hummed to you and stroked your precious face. I wanted my fingers to map out your perfect features and permanently tattoo themselves to my skin so that every time I felt lost, I could simply look down and know my way.

I did anything I could just get us through the horrific scene that filled that room, floor to ceiling. *This can't be happening. I just need to get us through...* To get us through the time it took for you to put on your angel wings and fly away to forever watch over us. I think that for years to come, it's okay for us to cry and allow the anger, guilt, and confusion to wash over us on your Angel-versary. After all, that day will always be one of the saddest and darkest days of my life. My sweet little miss taken from us. Robbed of all the experiences, and memories, and occasions we should have had. There will always be a missing face in the photos we take; I will see that empty space more than anyone else. A missing piece that fits the jigsaw puzzle that is my life. There will be no "first" incredible smile you bless us with, no "first" Christmas outfit, no "first" birthday cake, surrounded by your family looking upon you adoringly. So many "firsts" that have been stolen from me, and from you. That makes me so angry.

But I vow from today that for every year your birthday comes around, there will be no sadness. On that very special day, our hearts will be overflowing with joy, and love, because that memorable day, 26 February 2019, you changed our world as we know it. You changed the people we once were. My baby girl was born, and you deserve to be celebrated. It seems that there are three very significant versions of myself now. The me before you, the me when you rushed into my life, and the me that I am still trying to figure out since you went away. It's incredible how you can feel that change deep in your soul. I can never go back now. I am who I am now because of you, and that is what drives me to keep going forward. Through the tears, the pain, the loneliness, the laughter, the memories, my little miss; I will always go forward.

A letter from Brian...

Olivia-Grace: The world will never forget...

I came to the NICU twice during your short life, to see what beautiful being my friend had grown in her body, and I feel like you have been one of the most impactful little people I will ever meet. You will never know how sorry I am that your life was tragically cut short by means outside of anyone's control, and that you never got the chance to cuddle the huge plush elephant I bought for you, which upon returning home turned out to be your mother's teddy she held every night as she slept. I tried to be there for your mother as much as I could be, to support and help in any way, and I hope that all of us, those who truly loved you, can do you proud. I hope the world never forgets you; I know that I will never forget. As I sit and listen to a song by one of my favourite country artists, I think of you, and all that the lyrics mean. Sometimes there are no answers or reasons to be found, and we lose our special ones before their time. The world is made up of broken hearts, and broken halos. Your mother is one of my closest friends, we have a bond, and I am proud to say that every day I am reminded of you and your life.

Love to you, Olivia-Grace.

Brian

OLIVIA-GRACE
Please don't think I'll forget...

My mind is a maze of emotions, and my body is still reeling from the effects of pregnancy hormones. Throw in the depression that defines grief and you have one crazy, unstable "mother". Am I still allowed to call myself that? I don't know anymore. Some say yes. I question it. I'm not sure I feel like a mother anymore, so why call myself that? After all, it took nearly a whole week just for me to fully feel like your mummy, you know, to really *feel* it. That feeling came the day you crashed after being extubated. The doctors wanted you to try breathing on your own, but some hours later we got the dreaded knock on the bedroom door to tell us you were very poorly and needed re-intubating. You weren't ready to try, baby. I'm sorry we rushed you. I don't think I'll ever be able to forget how helpless I felt, standing at the end of your cot as one doctor performed CPR, another attacking your delicate veins with tiny needles, your pale skin already bruised from the cannulas, and the nurses adjusting the pumps that were giving you

45

drugs. *How could my baby be going through this? Be gentle with her!* All I could do was cup your small feet in the palm of my trembling hand, in the hope you would sense your mama was near and whisper through streaming tears, "It's okay, baby girl, Mummy's here." I'm not sure my voice made any kind of worthy sound, but I truly hope you could hear me, little miss. That was the moment a bang went off in my head, which sent ripples and electricity all down my shaking body. I was a mother. Your mother. I was watching you fight for your life and I've never known a feeling like this, to take over my entire body. I would die for you my love felt so great. Suddenly, for the very first time, everyone around me saw me for the true person I had become. And I had been waiting for you for so long. How have I not known you for forever? Now though, all I have are aching arms and an empty nest.

This thought is a frequent one I have. I miss you so much, but my want and need for a baby is still there. It's as though a very primal and instinctive role has taken over. I'm a new person, walking in new shoes now, and all I want is to learn how to become a mummy. But I have no one here to teach me. My heart literally hurts when I see other women smiling so sweetly at their own babies. I feel sick. I don't have the strength, or desire, to be around it. What cruel torture for my sodden and pained eyes to see it. I suppose some people may be shocked that such a thought would even cross my mind so soon after you were gone. It's okay though; let them be shocked. How can anyone else possibly understand a need so great? Even I'm confused. But the sad reality is that my eyes never stop looking for you. Looking for my baby. I want you here so badly, because I need to mother you. I need to mother. And so, when I think of the idea of another little person growing in my tummy, the only person I care about judging me, by appearing to "move on" and try again, is you.

Before anything else drastic happens in my life, my little miss, let me tell you this. You are my first baby. I loved you for every second of your life, and I will continue to love you for every last second of mine. Because of you I am no longer the same person, and in some ways, I am a better version of myself now because the unthinkable happened. When you died you forced me to show strength when I felt weak. You forced me to show my emotions, when before I had only wanted to hide them. I have more motivation now to save others and educate the world, because your life mattered. No one can make me think otherwise, and I will advocate and stand up for you until the day I die, I promise.

Five weeks is a short life, and I have come to realise that life cannot be measured by the physical years we possess, or our personal accomplishments. That no matter how small the footprint, the largest impact can be made on this Earth. Your death has already changed so much. So, when I think about having another baby, just know... You are irreplaceable. I will never, ever forget you. There is a piece of me only meant for you. But my arms are desperate and aching, and I'm searching the house for something I know isn't there. Because you live in my heart now, sweet little miss. Will you still love me, if I try to grow a new part of my heart for another little baby?

OLIVIA-GRACE
Mothers are so strong...

They say you have never experienced "real" love until your entire entity is overwhelmed with an unknown emotion as you hold your new baby's hand for the first time. Kiss their soft head for the first time. Then it hits you: *This is what they've been talking about! This is love!* I know this is true. I also know that no one knows what the love is like when you have to say goodbye to your child. That love measures a level of intensity I never knew possible. A level I hope not too many other mothers will ever have to endure. But, for some of us, the unlucky ones, we do have to endure it. We have to feel every emotion, the good, the bad and the ugly, that comes with giving birth to our baby, only to have to let them go. But it's quite amazing, isn't it? Through the worst time of my life, the days where I'm not sure how I'll go on and I'm sure my heart is about to stop, I somehow carry on living. Because the human race is founded on survival. We have to live. I truly believe that you beat the odds of surviving that first night and the coming weeks because of course you wanted to live. There was a purpose that you had to fulfil.

Grief is not optional; it's the price tag that comes with the gift of love. And when there is nowhere for that love to go, we grieve. We, and you, did not choose to stumble down this cold, dark and unsure road. But we were forced to, and so both strength and weakness became our friends, and we accept that the only way to live alongside grief is to grieve. Terminal, and only cured after a lifetime of missing you, until one day I will see you again. The days that are so dark and endless I call "my grief days". They don't need an explanation or justification; I just accept them for what they are. On these days, I have stayed horizontal in bed, watching meaningless videos on my phone, not even caring to shower to wash away the stench of my pain. I have cried oceans into my now permanently stained white pillowcase as I hold your teddy so tight that I'm afraid I'll hurt it in some way, as I listen to your lullaby over, and over, and over. "Baby Mine". From the *Dumbo* soundtrack. Such a beautiful song, for such a beautiful little girl. Those moments, when I allow myself the bittersweet memory of your photos and videos, I listen to you hiccupping. The most treasured sound my ears will ever hear. A sound that can never be recreated, because it came from deep within you. I feel kicks where you once slept in my belly, when I'm in that state. Is that normal to feel kicking when my body is truly alone? Is it you, sending me a sign that you are right there with me? I hope so… because I can really, honestly feel you. I have spent the evenings curled on the sofa, lost under a blanket, with a deep glass of wine. A drink I hope will temporarily numb my mind, body, and heart for just a few hours, because all my strength had simply been used up that day. I sometimes reach for my phone, wanting to connect with someone, but I don't know what to say or who to call. They don't know what to say. Sometimes it feels easier to be alone in my grief and just think of you.

But then, I have different days. My "doing days". In the evening, as I get ready for the task of sleep, I lie down feeling proud of myself, because on that day I was "doing it". I was "living it". Those days are like a break in the waves, a needed calm in the waters. I don't know how long the calm in this chaotic storm will last before the rain inevitably comes crashing down. But I know that for a brief time I can breathe, and I pause while the sun is shining. And so, on these rare days, I walk your big fur sister Naki, listening to the birds singing, feeling the spring breeze wrap around my neck, and I smile. You are there, carrying me in that moment. We have raised money for the transport team that got you to the NICU safely by baking scrummy cakes and sweet treats to enjoy. All displayed around the focal point of the table, your picture, radiating beauty and inspiration. That was a really good "doing it" day, little miss. People's generosity and giving warms my heart, and I know we are doing something wonderful for the world in your name. I need these days. Your grandma is already planning a fundraising event, to walk a bloody mountain! The money raised from that adventure will go to a charity focused on HIE research and support; anything we can do to help these beautiful little babies and the challenges they face. I talk to a nice woman called Sarah once a week. She is everything I imagine a counsellor to be; she wears a bright purple jumper and chunky beaded necklace, and she has an army of tissues ready to mop up my pain and live in the trenches with me. She has a tone to her voice that doesn't make me want to run away, and a gentle and soft smile that speaks *you're safe here*. We quickly arranged perinatal counselling once I got home from the NICU, empty-handed, already out of maternity clothes.

For me, I wanted to start this next chapter of living without you, because it was a chapter I knew was inevitably going to come, no matter how much I tried to turn the page backwards, and I knew I needed some guidance along the way. I don't know how this woman does it. Her ears and heart are so open and welcoming, to allow parents like me to ask her to carry some of our pain, if only for an hour. I feel comfortable sharing your pictures with her, and she speaks so fondly of the baby she never met. A small, windowless room. Just two ladies, and the army of tissues. It's a safe space to cry, but I mostly just love speaking your name so much, and of how proud I am of you. And of course, every other day, I sit at my laptop and do this. I write to you, I talk to you, I think of you and all we've been through together, and I am reminded that I am strong, brave, and bruised. I am here, protecting your memory and following my instincts, learning how to parent the dead. And I wonder what is to come...

"I see you everywhere, in the stars, in the river, to me you're everything that exists, the reality of everything."
Night and Day, Virginia Woolf

OLIVIA-GRACE
I'll make a wish for you...

*T*oday is my birthday, little miss. Quite a significant birthday, actually; I have reached the milestone age of thirty. I don't know what makes this particular birthday so special, or why over the years I have been counting down to it. I still haven't got my shit together and I look and feel older; little cause for celebration. It seems so obvious that I wouldn't want to acknowledge my birthday in any way, regardless of the age. I didn't open a birthday card or answer any calls. The idea of celebrating my birthday turns my stomach; it is not a happy day, and I do not feel happy. Making a birthday wish, where I could spend one more day with you, on a day where the sun never sets, is just a desperate fantasy. I'd trade in all my years to have the opportunity to give you a proper birthday party. And there my brain goes again, teleported into a make-believe universe where I imagine the balloons and dress you would have worn as we sang that special song for your very special first birthday. A parallel world where people's birthday wishes come true. A world where you and I are alive, together.

And today has been particularly hard and draining, and there have been tears. For the first time in a long time, I was so looking forward to this birthday, I was quietly excited. My dreams and wishes would have finally come true. But instead, those hopes have been shattered, right in front of my eyes in the most brutal way possible. Did I do something to deserve this? Am I being punished for a heinous crime I can't remember committing, and this is the way the universe is getting revenge on me? My brain is going off to a dark place again. I have spent the day alone, weighted down into my mattress, a broken woman's indent in the bed. I have not acknowledged it's the end of a decade, because I suppose I'm still so fearful of what's to come. What will my thirties hold for me? I ponder this thought as I let myself get tipsy on white wine, dressed in last night's pyjamas. A depressing thought to imagine another ten years passing me by, all the while missing the most precious gift I have ever been given. I've never been one for presents anyway, but even more so this year I actually feel repulsed by the idea of a gift. So as with the ignored calls, a small pile of neatly wrapped surprises sits waiting patiently in the corner of the room.

I don't want to seem ungrateful for my friends' and family's thoughtfulness, but right now I just don't care. The only gift I want is impossible. You can't go to a watch store and buy time with someone who no longer walks this Earth. There is no shop that sells a bottle of your delicious scent, as though it was a bottle of my favourite perfume. If they did, I would toss my classic Chanel in the bin, and I would wear you every day for the rest of my life. Never tiring of that smell. But I suppose that no matter what, when I look back to the last couple of years of my twenties, I will always find a smile and a glimpse of happiness hidden among the misery. Because that's when our story began together, my sweet baby girl. I met your daddy and I fell in love. And then like two pieces of a jigsaw puzzle, at exactly the right time when sparks were flying, you were made. And before the end of an era, I was the most blessed I could ever wish to be.

So, while I won't be laughing, or singing, or partaking in any traditional birthday antics, I will blow out a single candle, in the dark of my living room, alone, and I will make that birthday wish. I know you won't tell anyone, so it's okay that I say it out loud. My wish is that you, wherever you may be, are safe, and at peace. I hope you are dancing around the stars or are cruising a gentle current in the wind on a precious white feather. I hope the angels have healed you, and you are simply happy. Perhaps one day when we meet again, we will be written into a different story, with a different ending, and we'll get to spend a lifetime together. Our love is real and I believe it will find a way, and so I will impatiently wait until you're back where you belong. With me. But until that day, all I can do is love and miss you.

Immortality

(Do Not Stand By My Grave and Weep) by Clare Harner

Do not stand

By my grave, and weep,

I am not there,

I do not sleep

I am the thousand winds that blow,

I am the diamond glints in snow.

I am the sunlight on ripened grain,

I am the gentle, autumn rain.

As you awake with morning's hush,

I am the swift, up-flinging rush

Of quiet birds in circling flight.

I am the day transcending night.

Do not stand

By my grave, and cry

I am not there,

I did not die.

You came back to me today...

Like a kid at Christmas, filled with excitement and anticipation, I sat all morning by the front window, wide eyed and waiting. Waiting for the doorbell to ring, and for some stranger to hand me the most important parcel I have ever received. I can't tell you how fast my heart began to beat when I heard the songful charm of the doorbell. The most welcomed sound I have heard in a long time. Because in this package is a very special reminder. After you died, I knew I needed you with me at all times. Not just your spirit, close to my heart, but something physical I could gaze at and hold. We had chosen to have you cremated, and until now you were kept safe in a sweet and basic little box, next to my bed. I found a company called Ashes into Glass. They turn the ashes of your loved one into beautiful pieces of jewellery made out of gold and glass. And so that is what we did, little miss. You have been made into a beautiful, polished and engraved white-gold ring, with clear glass that reflects every speck of you. We travelled to the shop, your ashes were clasped tightly in my fist. No way was I going to put you anywhere other than in my hands. I was shaking as I passed you over so they could retrieve some ashes to make my ring. Such a small bag, for a small being. I don't know why I had expected more when you were sent back to me from the funeral home. You were so tiny. But when you see how little there is of your sweet baby, it's just heartbreaking. I was trusting my daughter with a stranger. An entirely different experience than I had previously thought I was going to have when someone else would be entrusted with your care. This wasn't daycare, or school, or even your first sleepover at Grandma's. This was a stranger, holding the ashes of my little miss.

The woman who took you was so kind and sympathetic. We were able to watch the glass-making process, and how they so lovingly incorporated you within this beautiful, glowing material. Careful not to waste a single speck. You would be returned to me fully, not a piece missing. I didn't want to wait for them to make my stunning white-gold ring, on the inside carved with the words *forever with Olivia-Grace*. I wanted you at that very moment. Time hits differently these days, and I knew waiting for you to come home would feel like an eternity. Do you know why it's tradition for women to wear engagement rings on their fourth finger, on their left hand? They say that the Romans believed that the vein that ran from that very finger traced all the way to the woman's heart. Because of this, they named the vein "Vena Amoris", the vein of love. Symbolic of the true love between two people. And I wear you extremely proudly on that finger. The unbreakable, undeniable chain of love between my own heart and you. A mother and her daughter. And every time I catch the sparkle of my new gift, the dashes of ash that remind me of the most stunning clear night's sky, I will remember you. I will remember the exact day you opened your eyes for the first time. 28 days old. But it was so worth the wait. I remember asking your grandma the question, "what if she lives, but never wakes up or opens her eyes? What if I never get to see her full face, or know who she will be?" I was so scared and overwhelmed by all of the unknown little miss, and not even the doctors could predict what the future may look like for us. But you did open your eyes; an incredible achievement and milestone that will fill me with pride for eternity. Your eyes were carved out of the most mystical and magical dark sky. They literally dazzled. I wonder if your future siblings will have your eyes. Your charm. I can only hope they take after you, with your strength, defiance, and beauty. But there will only ever be one pair of eyes that

can take my breath away and hypnotise me. And those are
your eyes.

A letter from Aunty Vanessa...

Olivia-Grace; Memories inside and out…

The morning was a crisp and fresh Tuesday in February, around 11 o'clock. I was off to take my dog Bella to the park, and I called your mama to see if she wanted me to take Naki too, as walking was getting a little hard and painful for her. But there was no answer; the phone rang and rang. I assumed your mama was just taking a nap, but as time went on, she didn't return my calls or read any of my messages, and something inside me started to feel "off".

Later that day, as I was driving home, I finally got a call from your mama. The details all melted into one as she told me the news. Considering your mama is a theatre nurse, I have never wanted a medical professional to be more wrong. I wanted her to have all the wrong information, and to be told that this was just one big mistake.

The words that struck me to my core, and I will never forget, were: "I will love her no matter what state her beautiful brain is in." In that moment I felt cold. Tears filled my eyes, distracting me from the road, so I did all I could think to do; I asked what I could do to help! I drove to a home you'll never know and picked up your fur sister. Naki would stay safe with me and Bella until your mama came home; that was my job. Never did I think for a second that when your mama did come home, it would be without you. I remember getting back home myself and thinking, why, what happened, why did it happen, why to your mama, why to one of my best friends? You read this stuff on social media or in news articles, but it doesn't actually happen to the people you know and care about! My heart ached for her, the pain in her voice, the strength of her soul scorned with lashings of fear and the unknown. At this point, I still thought everything would work out okay. Somehow, I thought the doctors and nurses would fix you, and you would be one of those stories of celebration as you made your grand exit from the NICU to venture home, a miracle recovery, and a miracle baby.

This was not the case, Olivia-Grace. Bad things happened, and weeks were spent by all of those who love you praying for your health. But the situation was so bad that your mama had to make an unthinkable decision to not allow you to live a life coated in pain and suffering. A lot of people called her brave. She was brave, and we all told her so, but that's not really the correct word, is it? Because what choice did she have but to be brave? She didn't feel brave living a life where there was no escape; she simply had to carry on and live with this torture.

The day you came back to your mama was in a way she never could have pictured, before all of this happened. I arrived at her house just after you had been delivered. A beautiful white-gold ring in the shape of a heart, wrapped around your ashes. You. She just wanted you close to her, the nearest thing she could get to a cuddle. The pain was bone deep around her eyes but she was so happy to be able to hold you in her hands. It was a strange but good thing to see her so excited about something at that time. But she was excited about something no one should ever be happy for. No child should have to be worn as jewellery, but how grateful we are that this was made possible, and a small token of comfort was found. I was happy for her, in the most unsettling way.

Some babies are too perfect for this world. A sentiment so graceful and beautiful, yet gut-wrenchingly awful, and wrong, and so (excuse my language, Olivia-Grace!) fucked up! I believe it, but it's still so, so wrong.

Love to you, Aunty V

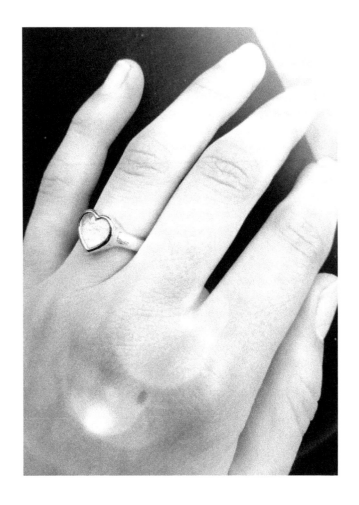

Olivia-Grace, my hand sparkles love and light
even on the darkest days

OLIVIA-GRACE
I'm getting awfully tired...

*T*hese past couple of weeks have not been good weeks. The waves have come so violently that I feel like I am drowning. I'm fighting for every breath, just trying to stay afloat. But grief has morphed into a weighted vest wrapped solidly around my chest, causing me to sink. On these days my eyes have been flooded with tears, my body soaked in alcohol, from simply trying to escape the dark and lonely evenings. I have cried so openly, honestly, and freely. Not angry tears anymore, just very sad ones. The kind that leaves a lump in your throat, a pain in your chest and stained streaks of grief, trickling down my cheeks. You simply cannot explain to friends, colleagues, strangers, how someone's heart can break over, and over, and over in one day. *Why me? Why me? Why my baby? Why did my baby have to die? It wasn't supposed to be like this. This wasn't supposed to happen.* Passing a woman, evidently pregnant, filled with hope and opportunity, right there in her swelling belly. Feelings that are mostly overlooked by the tiredness and general aches and pains of a pregnancy. Feelings I wish I had appreciated more. The cry of a newborn that somehow my senses can detect from what seems a mile away. The cry of wanting to be held and soothed by their mother. And my eyes fill to the brim. What I would have given to hear you cry out for me, little miss.

There is no "off" button to your brain. No "off" button to pain and loneliness. And these past couple of weeks have been harder, fuelled by shifting hormones and sleep deprivation.

I knew when I took that pill the doctor in the NICU gave me that my milk would soon dry up and my body would return to a pre-pregnancy state. There was no point in making food for a baby who wasn't here to eat it, and apparently, they have a pill for that. If only they had a pill to mend broken hearts, or better still, broken brains. Swollen boobs, throbbing and hot. Yet another stinging reminder that my body needed you, it was ready for you, and it was doing what it had been preparing for, and now it's all wasted. What a shitty cherry on top of a shitty cake, that our bodies are left with wounds and scars, saggy skin and stretch marks, and nothing to show off to the world and say, *I made that beautiful baby, my body did that.* I know how superficial I sound, but I'm just pissed off, Olivia-Grace. Mummy is mad.

I took the "dry me up" pill the day we left the NICU, almost an act of acceptance that you were leaving me and we were coming home alone. And I knew that within a month or so my body would be something new, and it would feel different again. Well, that was around eight weeks ago. And at 4 a.m. an unwelcomed familiar pain struck – my period was back, and for the first time in my life it brought not only physical annoyance and aches, but another sense of loneliness and a failing that I had never known before. It seemed a cruel reminder that I was not pregnant. It was just me, and no baby. My body is hollow, my body is empty. The sight of fresh blood made me break down in tears and sob heavily on the bathroom floor. Something that for over a decade I have lived with quite pleasantly and accepting of. My monthly reminder that my birth control was working, now makes me so angry that I ever had such a disillusion of how cruel and difficult life can be. Mad at my ignorance, once thinking that getting pregnant, staying pregnant and raising that baby was a given, no questions asked. Never considering that bleeding every month would cause a bleeding heart. Today, and for every day, a new community of women will forever be in my thoughts and prayers. I hear you now. I see you.

I've never experienced a void so deep that could only be filled by one thing. The one thing I can't have. There are days when I think I can still feel you wiggling about inside me, kicking to let me know you are there. My brain is playing tricks on me. The throbbing ache for you so intense I can feel it in my bones, never to let up. And so, this week I have been very tired. Tired from it all, and simply missing you every second of every day. It's exhausting and harrowing knowing there is no relief from that feeling, and suddenly my life seems like it will last such a long, long time. I don't wish for death, baby girl, to finally receive some respite; please don't think that. Dying wouldn't do the cause for my living much good, would it? But I am no longer afraid of death. I have purpose and belonging both Earthside and in Heaven. But until now, I realise, I have never really, truly missed someone. This feeling is relentless. There is no comfort to be sought, to dampen the pain that is missing you. Did I make the most of the time we had together? Did I sing to you enough, and hold your precious feet as many times as I could in one day? Did you know my whole heart belonged to you from the minute I found out I was pregnant with you? I suppose it's normal to feel like I didn't do any of that stuff enough. How could there possibly be "enough", if I already knew you'd leave me forever? An entire lifetime of hugging, kissing, and loving you would still not be enough for me. I hate that I will never know the person that you would have become, and I hate that I will never know who I would have become with you. I hate that these thoughts play over, and over, and over again in my head. I hate that there are times when I catch myself crying without even realising. Staring at my own reflection in the mirror as I watch the tears fall, knowing that this raw, damaged, and hurt girl looking back at me doesn't have a damn clue what she is doing. I just feel so hateful and lost right now. How am I still here when I feel like a dead soul walking among the living? But I am trying to live, little miss. I'm always trying, because you deserve to have a mother who is strong for you. After all of your courage and bravery, I know that I need to honour you by living in the same way.

A letter from Aunty Holly...

Olivia-Grace; Another piece to my family...

As soon as I found out you were snuggled up in the tummy of my tattooed, pencil-skirted twin, I fell in love with you. I had my first cuddle already planned out in my head. You would call me Aunty Holly, or "Holls", as your mummy calls me, and you would be my Jasmine's friend, a niece and cousin not by blood but by something even stronger: love.

And then you were here. All of a sudden, this stunning little being. You transformed from a bump into a beautiful baby girl, and my best friend became a mother. And this she will always be. Whether you are here in her arms or locked away in her heart, you never stop being a mother.

While you were in your mummy's tummy, I wrote her a poem. I wanted to give her any advice and helpful words that I could about the wonder of motherhood, and how I had watched her grow these last seven months. Those words will stay with me alone now, because nothing I could have said would ever have prepared her for the journey you were both about to share.

You stole a piece of my heart the second I laid eyes on you, with your rosebud lips, long feet and the most mesmerising eyes any of us have ever seen, and your own unique, beautiful soul. You squeezed my finger as I read to you, but in the end, you went away, and our worlds collapsed. Such a short time you were here but what an impact you made.

You were meant for something far greater than this world, Olivia-Grace, and my heart will never forget you.

Aunty Holly

OLIVIA-GRACE
It's a girl!...

Some hours are lost ignoring the outside world, where I go back through my phone from the very beginning, fixated on your memories. The very first picture that started our story together seems like a lifetime ago. I looked so young, my eyes shining bright and so blissfully excited as I exposed my bare, slim stomach, and the words "five weeks pregnant" displayed, written in red lipstick. I can't help shaking my head, pitying the happy girl I see in the photo for what she is going to have to live through. I look back at one particularly special and raw video. This video encapsulated nothing but love and excitement. The day that big black rubber balloon popped in front of our family and friends, and a shower of pink confetti rained to the floor. "It's a girl!" I cried, I screamed, I jumped in the air – but you already know that, don't you, little miss? You heard me, you felt my body leap off the ground. I already had an instinct that you were a little girl. I felt tuned in to you from

74

the day I took that test, but until I knew for sure, I was too afraid to believe it.

To see the colour pink, to know I would have a daughter, sent me euphoric. I had always dreamt of having a daughter, and to see what my future may hold in a colourful stream around my feet made my heart grow ten sizes with pure love and thrill. That will be one of the happiest moments in my whole life. And I am so glad that I remember that feeling so vividly, even if it is bittersweet now. I look back at that video and watch with a pounding heart, rosy cheeks and glistening eyes... I was so filled with hope back then. *I was so happy...* And I cry. I cry because I miss you. I cry because back then I knew nothing of what we were about to face. I cry because I regret the amount of strength you had to show from the minute you were born. And I cry because I love you. I love you so much. But the smile I see looking back at me is one of the most genuine smiles you will ever see painted on a person's face. I knew you were there, waiting patiently and growing. I felt you; we were merged together by the most wonderful and unique bond. You were a true part of my body, and because of that I smiled.

I am different now. There is no "girl from the photos" anymore, one so blissfully unaware. The voices are loud in my mind. I doubt myself, I doubt faith and trust, I find doubt in everything around me. But then I remember you, and I am pulled back to this reality. I am reminded that I am so in love with you, and for that reason alone I am blessed. I silence those voices and delete any doubt, and I tell myself I need to be strong. I will be strong. And I remember your beauty. But I am tired, little miss. I'm tired and I want to sleep a dreamless sleep. I dream of you a lot, and while we have vanished into a special dream place, it feels so magical. But it's like a cruel game my own mind plays on me. You're so close, but I can never fully have you. And then, of course, I have to wake up. I wake up to fight the same war that is life with grief, that had left me so tired the night before. I suppose that defines bravery. I wake up to a quiet empty house, no baby crying or fussing waiting to be fed. And then it's time to go back to the battlefield.

"It's no use going back to yesterday, because I was a different person then." Alice in Wonderland, Lewis Carroll

OLIVIA-GRACE
I made a new friend today...

*T*oday, I was very brave. Today I had my alarm set to make sure I was up and out of the house by 10 a.m, with Naki by my side for emotional support and courage. I went and joined a bereavement group for morning coffee. I was so scared as I walked into the cafe. Heart pounding and beads of sweat trickling down my neck. As I walked up to a welcoming face, nametag on and a smile painted on her face, the familiar lump in the back of my throat caught me off guard. I really had to fight back tears after I had introduced myself and she asked the dreaded question... "Who have you lost that has brought you here today?" I had tried to mentally prepare for this kind of introduction, and I had practised the answer over and over in my head so that I wouldn't choke on the disgusting words I had to respond with, *my baby,* but how can I even speak when those words steal my breath away? Innocent questions stab my wounded heart and I just don't know how to answer. There is no easy question these days. Even, *how are you doing?* sends me into a confused panic. *I don't know how I'm doing, I just*

know everything hurts. My hands were sweating and my stomach may as well have flipped down to my pants as I somehow whispered, through a crackling voice and the feeling of daggers in my chest "...*My little girl...*" My gosh, that was hard. I knew that doing something like this would be hard, but I never imagined I would feel so afraid. I guess I was afraid of being vulnerable around people I didn't know. I was afraid of their pity. All of these strangers would look at me and know my heart was breaking. There is nowhere to hide in a room full of people overcome with loss. They don't know my story, and they don't know yours, but they do know I am in pain. Just as they are. It doesn't matter who you have lost; the age, the gender, the relationship you once had with that invisible soul, or how long that person blessed your life with their simple being; the pain is just as real for every one of us in that room. And you can feel it. It's in the air, written on aged faces, the undertone of the general chit chat. Pain is all around.

I know no one expected me to be there because I had lost a child. The grief of baby loss is so complex and impossibly isolating. I was the only person in that room who sat timid and shy in this shitty club of *bereaved parent.* I had been made aware that there was a specific group, local to me for the parents of this club. But truthfully, I am not ready. I'm not ready to sit in a room and bare my soul and story, surrounded by *that* level of heartbreak. I know the support is there, and when I am ready, I will pack your teddy in my bag for an extra ounce of bravery, put on layers of waterproof mascara, and I will cry among other loss mums. But today, this is all I can do. And that is more than okay. Support and comfort can be found in the most unusual places, and as an older lady sits holding my hand, I do feel comforted. A room of strangers that I'll probably never see again, who glance at me with a nervous half smile to invite the opportunity of a conversation, made me feel as though, despite the pain or who we were missing, we were going to face this grief journey together. We would brave the pain together. Everyone absolutely adored Naki. She was such a good girl. Waddling around the room, lying down for belly rubs by the old women's feet, or sitting next to the chair of an older chap, painting the true and loyal picture of man's best friend. She brought so many smiles today. In fact, I don't think I could have done today without her. She helps to make me feel just a little bit stronger, and when my hands start to tremble, she knows to nuzzle her wet nose into my body and remind me that I am safe. She is used to attention; being a perfect Corgi she tends to attract the admiration of everyone who passes her and her short stumpy legs and soft fox ears, but it was as though she knew how much these strangers needed her as well, today. And she was more than happy to comply.

I am trying to be so very strong for you, little miss. I hope you took a little trip with me today, Olivia-Grace. I hope you heard me talk so sweetly and so proudly of you. Even though I miss you, and I still feel so empty, it really is hard not to have the biggest smile on my face when I talk about your beauty and incredibly inspirational character. How did you get to be so wonderful? How is it fair that life took away such a precious gem? I suppose a similar question is asked many times, by every one of these special people in this group; a wife without her husband, a daughter without her father, a boy without his grandmother, and of course, me without you.

OLIVIA-GRACE

Will the pain tear us apart...

I'm scared, Olivia-Grace. I'm scared I'm losing your daddy. It's so hard when two people are hurting in such magnitude; it's near on impossible to be each other's support system. Especially when men and women are worlds apart in every which way, in matters of the mind, heart and soul. Am I losing him to grief? Losing him to the distance we have had to endure, through the times we needed each other the most? Losing him through the challenge that is accepting our baby girl is gone? He was very supportive when we were in the hospital, both scared senseless and trying to understand what the doctors were telling us. But he can't feel what I'm feeling. It's impossible. I can see his frustration with not fully understanding me. Understanding what my body has truly gone through after pregnancy, birth, and the postpartum struggles. He is frustrated and so am I. Am I grieving too slowly for him? *Please, don't rush me, please.* I need a mind reader right now, a rock, a constant, and that is a lot to ask of someone. But I need him, because I cannot bear

81

this grief alone, though I am trying. I promise I am doing the best I can. Perhaps I am being selfish. I've never done this before, so I don't know how to ask for help, or what exactly it is that I even need from him. I can read all the baby and birth books, all the grief books, yet now I have become the statistic, and I still feel as though I have to figure it out alone. I ask myself, does he still love me? Does he still love me as his partner, or as the mother of his child? Does he remember all the times we laughed together, cried together, made memories together? The thing that scares me the most is that he is the last physical thing, with a steady, solid beat of a heart, that truly connects me to you. You are a part of myself and Daddy, made from the love we had for one another. Our DNA intertwined, interconnected, to create the most precious thing on this planet. With dark hair, a Mongolian blue spot on your bottom, and eyes that lit up our world.

But I suppose now we have become different people. Am I ready now, to venture through life without him beside me, helping me along the way? Has my capacity for love grown so much that my own hugs are enough to soothe my aching heart and soul? I pray for him to grieve for you in a healthy way that doesn't push us apart as a couple. I pray for him to say your name, so loudly and so proudly, but I see him turning away from that challenge; throwing himself into the normality of life, I suppose, to get him through the day. I don't want him to pretend you never existed, because it's the easier route than facing what we're going through. And when we're asked the dreaded question by innocent strangers about our family, I don't want him to pretend that we are still living in a time when it was just me and him. I pray for him to answer this very question with the response *yes*. "Do you have any children?" Head held high, a smile on his face, and the words; "Yes. I have a daughter. Her name is Olivia-Grace, and she lives in my heart now." Maybe he is just afraid too. Maybe, the way I stumble and trip on well-meaning questions and conversation, he does too. I know he loves you so very much, baby, please don't ever think otherwise. I won't allow anyone to ever think otherwise. He did everything he could do for you, and for me, to the best of his ability. But life now with you gone... well, life is new again, and his world is so very different to mine. You were here, you lived, you existed, and I'm choosing to keep you present with me. I pray he chooses to keep you present with him too. Our daughter. I suppose, my little miss, I will simply continue to pray...

OLIVIA-GRACE
I'm not okay...

I don't really have anything to say. My fingertips just hover quietly over the keyboard, because I want to feel close to you somehow. Today is just a day. The stages of grief come and go, so erratically and so unorganised, like the weather; I can't keep up with them. They're winning, and they completely and relentlessly own me. I'm learning that grief follows no rules. She's her own boss, and she likes to tease and play with her forever guest, catapulting from phase to phase, some moments just a taste, and others she unpacks and sets up home. I don't want to scream, cry, eat or sleep, talk, or try and process the thoughts and feelings that cause me to drown. My brain knows you are dead, but my heart does not, and I miss you so damn much it hurts. With every aching beat of my heart that whispers *I remember you*, it physically hurts. I'm just not okay, and that is all. Is it alright if I just sit here silently, with grief, welcomed but unwanted, and just be "not okay"? Just for a while...

Olivia-Grace, hold my hand little miss, I'm just not okay

OLIVIA-GRACE
Another twist, another turn...

*T*oday is the start of a new chapter. Not too long after you left us here alone, your daddy left me. My feelings of what was to come were right, as I watched him slip away and admit to himself that this new reality was not one he could be a part of. Another blow to an already difficult and ever-changing life, and some new layers of grief to add to our story. Grief became too much. Grief, a simple basic word that doesn't do the complexity and damaging effects any kind of justice. It all just got too much. Of course it did, because our love for you was and is so great. With that kind of love, the pain has to be equally as magnificent. I suppose in some way he forgot. Forgot his love for me, and the promises he made to both his girls. Emotionally drained and falling out of love, and now we are both single people, with only an angel baby.

When you don't feel like the same person anymore, no one around you seems the same either; everyone is a stranger. Everything you see, hear, feel becomes so tiresome and heavy, you drown in it. It's an overwhelming

86

load to bear when there is just no mental, emotional, or physical energy left.

These eyes don't belong to the girl he once met. My skin is a different shade of pale, worn-out, and broken. But don't for one second believe that this choice he made reflects in some way that he didn't love you. Because he did. And as I've told you before, you were made from love. When life was good, the sun was shining, and we were happy. But life isn't always like that, little miss. Life gets hard, and our hearts break from trauma and loss. I wish things had been different. I will always be so grateful to him for letting me steal a piece of his heart and co-creating the best thing in the world. I'll miss his smile for a lifetime, and the way he made me feel so safe, and I hope he takes some precious memories of me with him, wherever he may end up. But I can't cling on to someone else when I'm using all of my energy to hold and protect you so tightly.

I wish perhaps I hadn't been such an unbearable load to support and care for. My emotions, sleep deprivation, hormones, rage, uncontrollable and spontaneous outbursts of tears and screams have become too much to handle for those around me. All of my relationships now seem to be smeared with this tragedy and have put such a strain on them; I'm feeling like most of them won't survive. I'm asked by those close to me, when they see me spiralling, *how can I help? What can I do?* But I don't have any answers for them. I don't know what they can do to support me through living with baby loss. Instead, they just have to watch me suffer, because nothing anyone can do can fix my life now or make things better. I never knew how impossibly lonely this journey would be. The feeling that no one understands me at all, and I can't find the words to explain the debilitating waves of every grief emotion that I feel in almost every waking moment. I try to communicate as best I can, but grief has slurred my words and emotions into an incoherent mess, and I worry I'm pushing people away with the frustration of trying to care for me. I worry I'm losing everything.

I do have a handful of true friends who are my pillars, and thankfully I don't have to question them staying put in our lives, despite this version of me being incredibly hard work. They let me break, with no judgment, and carefully pick up the trail of my broken pieces to store carefully and put back together, only when the time is right. But your daddy and I are finding our ways on paths that have strayed further and further apart, and now there is an ocean between us. An ocean, and a galaxy of different emotions and coping strategies. So here is another promise that I will make to you, my sweet angel baby. Like the pain of letting you go consumed my every fibre, I never gave up. And like this new change in my life will be so very hard and tiring, I will still never give up. I have survived 100 percent of my worst days, and so I will survive this. I will not allow myself to become cold and distant. I will not shy away from the intense, pulsing beat of my heart when I think of you. I will not allow another trauma to break me, when I have already gone through the worst thing a person, a mother, can go through. I am terribly sorry for how this all played out. I wish that as the special anniversaries and occasions come around, we'd be united in strength and love to get through them together and to honour you in some way, but that can't happen now. I could go over it and over it in my head, to try and understand, rationalise, sympathise even, but it wouldn't change anything. I'm here now, without you, and without him, but somehow you keep reminding me that I am not alone.

"Things are sweeter when they're lost. I know because once I wanted something and got it. It was the only thing I ever wanted badly. And when I got it, it turned to dust in my hands." The Beautiful and Damned, F. Scott Fitzgerald

Half a year is a long time...

*H*appy half-a-year birthday, my sweet little miss. As the days, weeks and months pass me by, time does not become distance. You are not further from my mind and heart just because the hours continue to spin around the clock. Six months does sound like such a long time though, yet to me, everything that happened was just yesterday. It's today. It's right now. Does grief warp time this noticeably? Is that why the memories, feelings and crushing waves of anxiety are stored in such a present place that it only takes the slightest thing to pour out in an unregulated outburst? I feel as though I am still living in that moment; I can't escape it and nowhere feels safe. Birth trauma and PTSD, I will never understand you, and I don't want to.

Today, the sun shines brightly, and the trees smell so fresh, but I find myself sobbing out on the forest floor by your grandma's house, as I'm feeling the same pain I felt the day I let you go. That sharp, unmistakable stabbing in my chest that only comes when I think of you and what should have been. My tainted soul that now knows that seeing two pink lines does not mean a baby at home. I tried so very hard to be brave for you. To wear a smile for you, around all of your aunties and uncles who came to me, to love and support me on this day. Six damn months.

But as I sit alone, needing that time to gather myself before meeting everyone, and I look through your photos, I have a hurricane-like hit of panic. What happens when I run out of photos to share? When I've memorised every last detail of each picture, and I need something new to scratch the itch you left behind? And I'm angry again. We don't get the chance to make any more memories, do we? I can't take your picture ever again, as you look up at me so innocently. Your eyes lost, but I know you were searching for me. Blind, they said. Most likely, due to the brain damage you would have been blind. But you don't need to see my face to know who I am. You don't need to see anything to know your whole life was simply spent being loved. Days like these, the confusing need for another baby is just overwhelming; the feeling frightens me. Is it only me that can literally see a black space that runs in between my arms, crying out for a little person to cradle and rock? I've become fixated with these empty spaces. The space on my body, beside my breast, the corner in my room where your cot lay waiting and ready, forever to be unfilled and unknowing of the sweet smell of a baby, the empty space in the back seat of the car... The list goes on. I see it everywhere. But I suppose the truth is, what I really need I can't have. What my soul is yearning for is another chance with you.

I want to go back and start that day over again. I would have gone to the hospital earlier. I should have known my body better. I should have gone earlier, when the pain became a warning sign of something tragic happening. *I should have gone sooner*. Demanded they get you out of me as fast as possible. *Cut me open, I don't care, just keep my baby safe*. I'm sorry, Olivia-Grace. I'm sorry, I'm sorry, I'm sorry. My breath is getting thick, tight, and fast, my eyes clamped shut, yet they still overspill with tears of acid, and I am so lost again, and it hurts so damn much. I try my best, but there are just some days when there is no peace to be found. You're gone. And I am here. And it's all wrong.

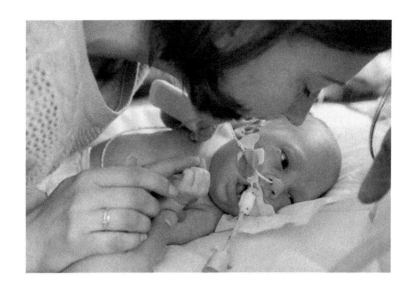

Olivia-Grace, I could gaze upon your face for an eternity

OLIVIA-GRACE
It's still the same inside...

People don't see the same things when they look at me these days, little miss. From the outside, I look almost like a regular woman, living a regular life, free from pain, trauma, and loneliness.

I wonder why society puts an expiry date on grief? I'm sure they don't mean to, but the expectation is there for sure. A subconscious timeline set by other people who, after a certain point, expect me to have "moved on". What a privilege it is for these people who expect me to be okay, to not actually understand what losing a baby feels like. Maybe I fool them. Maybe we all see what we want to see, to avoid uncomfortable and hard conversations. My pain does seem to make others uncomfortable. Some days it just seems easier to fake a smile and have them believe I am in fact doing "okay". You can't see tears behind sunglasses, after all. The truth is, grief has many different invisible faces that wear me daily, hourly, sometimes just for a second. I keep loss secrets now, because I can't bear the person I would be known as if I say them out loud. My own thoughts are so terrible, they scare me. Where has my empathy gone? My patience, tolerance and understanding? Traits that once made me, me. A good person, I think. Dani. I've been bulldozed into tiny pieces, jumbled up and messily put back "together".

Some days, I have so much rage I simply hate everyone around me for not having to suffer this tragic life. When I know that someone is trying to conceive, I hide the disgusting thought deep within me that I hope they can't get pregnant, so I don't have to see or hear yet another pregnancy and birth announcement, and the conflicting emotions that come along with it. I just want to be happy for them and their good fortune and excitement, but I ask myself, why? *Why, why did we not get a happy ending to our story?* I hate myself. The insane jealousy I feel when a rain of pink falls from a gender reveal balloon. I had been praying it was blue, just so it would be a little bit easier on my heart. I was never a bad person. But has grief turned me into a monster?

Sometimes grief becomes all of me and she can be a real bitch. The worst one though, please forgive me, little miss, is sometimes… *I'm so sorry*... I wish they hadn't been able to bring you back. Sometimes I wish I didn't have all the traumatic memories of the things I saw, smelt, and heard in those five weeks we were together. I think maybe, if my fate had already been decided that I would lose you, would it have been "easier" if you were born already sleeping? No wires, no tubes, no testing with big, scary machines, no decisions to be made. There's that bitch again. I hate her. How could I possibly think this? Surely I don't mean it. My senses come back to me and I realise that it doesn't matter when you lose a baby; for that mama who saw two pink lines, she has become one with her child, a beating heart inside her body, and created a love that can never be replicated.

You were born still and your heart had already stopped, the damage already done, but you were not ready. Nothing would have made losing you "easier", but I think sometimes my brain looks for an escape, a moment of bargaining that may give respite to the exhausting memories. So, I quickly force that thought to the deepest, darkest place within me, lock it away, and remember you blessed me with time. Only a tiny bit, but we had time. And in that time, we made memories, and we grew our bond over stories, songs, and cuddles, and I choose to remember. Those memories, no matter how difficult they are for my heart to carry… Well, it doesn't mean they are bad. Quite the opposite. I do treasure those traumatic yet beautiful memories. Like the day you opened your eyes for the first time. I think I spent a moment in Heaven. Leaning into your cot and singing Disney songs to you, while I just watched you breathe. When you peed right into the bare hands of the doctor, pay back for sticking you with a needle! I truly laughed that day. It had been so long since I had laughed, so thank you. And so, I tell that ugly side of grief to piss off, and send a kinder version of herself to me. Sometimes she listens, other times I have to be a little more patient and wait for her to move on in her own time. I just plead with her, no matter what I think or feel sometimes, don't take those memories from me… *you've already taken so much.*

A letter from Nay...

Olivia-Grace; A poem for you...

Just wanted to check in, its Aunty Nay here,

There's something I wanted to say, now let me be clear,

That I, and so many others, hold you so dear,

And wish with all my being, that you were still here.

If you were here, I'd spoil you rotten,

Through us, your soul is never forgotten,

To stroke your soft head, made me so glad,

Envious of your strength, that I wish I had.

Eyes the colour of a twilight sky,

And beyond that sky you will always fly,

And a new moon will not go by,

That our little miss does not bring a tear to our eye.

And now you are as safe as can be,

From a world that wasn't worthy,

So, when I see spring daffs and a buzzing bee,

The image of you, that will forever stay with me.

We love you in the strongest way, and you're forever in my heart.

Love, Nay

OLIVIA-GRACE
Back to work...

It's been more than four months now since you passed, and the days and nights have blurred into one. I don't even know what the date is! Days have merged into weeks, and weeks into months, and I'm shocked at how warped time has become. Another unusual change I'm trying to adjust to; time doesn't feel the same anymore. There has been no alarm startling me out of bed in the morning, no wind-down evening, relaxing bath and bedtime to look forward to; my days are endless and unorganised, and that's what grief is all about. But I need some routine and a purpose in rolling my butt out of bed in the morning. So, I met my boss for coffee and a chat. A boss who doubles as a friend, who was at your funeral, and I knew, whatever I needed to help me transition into this next phase, he would make it happen.

The thought of going back gave me anxiety, as I tried to imagine how I would trick my brain into functioning as a semi-sane and "normal" person. I work in the very building I delivered you in. Just down the hallway in fact. I know the hallways, the faces, the smells, the different alarms echoing down the corridor, distant in the neighbouring department. *Beep, beep…* that's another emergency in the ICU. I'm not afraid that I can no longer do my job in the clinical skills aspect of it all. I'm good at my job, and I have a passion for it. But I am afraid that I can't do my job anymore because of the emotional investment it requires. Can I bandage myself up well enough to help piece another person back together? To help them recover? To help them live? To comfort, and ease the nerves of a terrified patient? I used to be so good at hand-holding and connecting with my patients. Can I go back to being in love with my job and the difference I got to make, when these days the only thing that I love sits in a memorial box on my bedside table illuminated by a single candle?

And I am afraid that I don't know anyone there anymore. Or more so, they don't know me. I imagine walking into the coffee room, a cosy room that buzzed with the smell of coffee and friendly chit chat. I look almost the same as I once did, slim frame and tattooed arms, under royal blue scrubs and an unflattering theatre cap, but I'm not a permanent member of staff here. I'm just an imposter in a uniform, a visitor. *I don't belong here anymore.* The last time I sat in this coffee room I had a huge bump filling out my shirt. I relaxed on my break, enjoying a piece of homemade cake supplied by a gracious doctor who had the delicious hobby of baking, and you were kicking with pleasure and a sugar rush. I'm not that Dani anymore. I'll be met with a sea of sympathetic faces, familiar, yet it feels as though I'll be meeting them for the first time, and I'm scared.

Well, the day quickly came around, and my alarm did startle me out of bed; it's been so long since I've had to listen to that horrible noise, and 6 a.m. feels very, very early. Did I even sleep the night before? As I got myself up, I did a quick mental self-check to determine whether today was going to be a "grief day" or an okay one, and I could decide from there whether or not I could take the plunge and go back to work. My first day as the "new Dani" that everyone would meet and work alongside. I would not push myself, and my boss knew this. Huge steps and courage are needed to return to a hint of a previous life; it has to be when I'm ready, or I will fail. We agreed I would start on a very slow and gentle phased return, with constant support and review from management and occupational health, a plan I felt was fair and achievable, and these days I have learnt not to put unnecessary pressure on myself. I do only what I can do. And on the morning of my "first day", to my surprise, I didn't feel too nervous, I only felt tired. So, time to make myself look semi-decent, and head off to work. I had already mentally mapped out my entry route into my department so I could avoid trigger spots, as I know now PTSD strikes in those painfully memorable places, but I had a focus in mind, so getting through those front doors was actually easier than I expected. I was grateful for that. I had no idea the physical toll six hours of work would take on my body. By the end of my shift I had a banging headache, my body felt heavy and my feet had forgotten how getting comfy in clogs takes time and practice. Physically and mentally, at the end of my short work day, I was completely shattered. I came home and I slept. I know not every day will be like this, a tiring success in regaining some structure to my messy life. There will be challenges along the way that I can't prepare for, but for now, I had a good day and I remind myself, you will help me get through anything.

My colleagues were fantastic. I had a few warm cuddles, and secret tears hidden behind face masks, but mostly people talked to me without fear or anticipation; they were happy to see me. They let me take control over conversation and lead it to a place I felt comfortable and safe, and quickly gave me an easy exit route if they could sense I was beginning to feel too vulnerable and overwhelmed with it all. Of course, they all have questions. I can hear the words unspoken. But for today, I think they were just glad to see me surviving.

OLIVIA-GRACE
Am I dreaming...

I sometimes wonder if everyone feels as though this last year was simply a bad dream. Surely this can't have happened to their daughter, their friend, their colleague? Are we sure this was real? While I'm left paralyzed, sinking into my pit of grief, the world moves on. It seems so long ago now; it mustn't have been real? I wonder, have they really forgotten you? But we both know that this last year is far from a dream. Pregnancy, birth, and death. A dream I have awake and asleep. But this living nightmare is one that doesn't just go away, because I look so "normal". My face paints a picture that others need to see. I smile, I laugh, I work, and I play. But deep inside me, within the black void that remains constant, a dull yet intense ache is still very much my reality. I still think about you every second of the day. Looped on repeat, my perfect angel baby and your sweet pretty face. I still yearn to talk about you and say your name, as though your body is still present here on this Earth. Saying your name keeps you alive, and I'll do anything to keep you alive. *Please ask me her name*, I beg silently to myself. I cling to every last inch of your blanket, wishing for the smell to never fade away. I don't think people have forgotten, and I am eternally grateful to those who simply walk beside me on this grief journey, putting no end date on my pain. True friends to me, and to you.

But I don't think that my face is painted with the same grief that it was a few months back. I wore that pain like war paint. And it was so obvious. But perhaps now, as time continues to pass us by, you've settled into the grooves of my aged face, to be worn as subtle daytime make-up. Grief is ever evolving, ever changing. But when I look in the mirror, I see something entirely different to that of other people, looking back at me. I see someone who looks a lot like me, but I get lost searching her face. I want to reach through the glass and touch her, to make sure she is real. I'm curious, as I recognise the features of this familiar girl, but now we are unsure of each other. I see a mother, longing and pining for her baby. The unseeable spaces that scream for you, that have latched onto my body, and the desperate need to fill the empty space within my arms, close to my chest. I see a broken heart, that with love, support and time is slowly being patched back together, always to remain damaged, but to beat a little stronger than the day before. And I see a warrior. A warrior that bears a form of strength, only to be experienced when you birth your child, and you kiss a final goodbye to them. Some days I want to look up to the stars that you have polished to shine so brightly, and shout at the top of my lungs, *I'm doing it, Olivia-Grace! Mummy is still here, and I am still so in love with you. Because of you, I am living!* I know you know this, little miss. I do know...

A letter from Aunty Hayley...

Olivia-Grace; I'll gaze at you...
It's hard to hear it,
It's hard to say it,
It's hard to believe it,
It can only be harder to live with.
It's like looking into the dark abyss of the infinite universe, and spotting a star so dazzlingly bright. For a second everything falls away and nothing is real, realising everything is just energy, existing at the same time.

You are our star. Your life was brief, and your loss will be felt deep within us, until we are gone. But you'll shine through as hope and love, until the end of time.
Endless love, Aunty Hayley

Olivia-Grace, our sweet little miss. Our Wonder Woman

OLIVIA-GRACE
We took a trip...

I need a break. Grief has worn me down, and I'm craving an escape. We planned a trip away for a long weekend, to enjoy the last of the summer sun before the new season sends the cold air and rain, and paints a canvas of oranges and reds as the leaves fall to the ground. I have been working, interacting, and functioning; I'd even go so far as to say I smile again now, but I still feel far from living a life I once knew. A life that didn't require such daily effort, self-check-ins, and weekly therapy. The people around me don't see just how much work I am actually doing. The world is moving on and people are living their own life. I do a good job of hiding the erratic waves of grief behind closed doors, washing them down the steamy shower drain or silencing them under the stuffy heat of my weighted duvet, for fear of becoming a burden to those around me. And so frequently I cry alone and quietly. If I do disclose that I'm struggling with something, the response is usually kind, but hurried now. Unsure of what to say to someone who should be an experienced griever by now, under the illusion that so many months have passed, surely my pain has subsided and I have adjusted to my new reality. I hate it when people say to me... *"It will take time, but you will get back to normal."* No. No, I will not. I wish people wouldn't put that pressure and unrealistic expectation on me; I wish they wouldn't think that I could ever possibly return to a place I used to be in, that once felt "normal". That this debilitating thing called a broken heart could possibly fade away with time, as though the love I have for you, my daughter, will also fade away. This, this is my new normal... for now. I know it will change, like the promise of new seasons, but I will never go back to the place I came from.

God, I hate that word these days. Normal. What the fuck is normal anyway? My understanding of grief is growing and I'm learning that I hold you carefully in my heart, and weathered hands, and my life is growing around you. You will never shrink within my palms, and I will always cup and protect you, but as grief continues to shift and change, so do our lives. The grief itself does not diminish. This fairy tale belief that time heals all wounds? Bullshit. They're waiting for me to be "okay", to "get over the trauma of losing you", and dare I say it... "move on". They think they are being patient with me, waiting for me to wake up one morning without the soul and heart of a loss mum. *The old Dani is back!* But instead I think, how kind would it be if people took the time to get to know the new me? Every day until the day I die, I will wake up in the morning as a loss mum. I know these triggering and insensitive comments come from a good but unknowing place. A place they think will motivate and encourage me, to not let myself become consumed and defined by my loss; but honestly, I want to tell them to shut up about things they know nothing about.

Our bags packed, a fiercely loyal friend and I began the drive to Wales. We were escaping, and dared to enjoy a weekend of fun and frolicking. There was some kind of sparkle in the air between us as we drove away from the home of my heartache. I had thought about going abroad for the guarantee of burning heat and unlimited drinks, but somehow the idea of leaving the country and my safe spaces made me feel as though I would be even further from you. So, I found a beautiful holiday house for us, lost down a narrow country road, surrounded by rolling green hills and the smell of trees and the song of birds. The security of knowing your teddy was packed in my bag, to spend the nights cuddled up with me, made the trip easy. I did promise to take you on my adventures, didn't I?

We explored this idyllic place, and I immersed myself in the excitement of something new. I found myself wearing a smile and laughing more often than not this weekend, as we hiked, canoed and tasted local beers in the village pub. And though you were never far from my mind, I think I'm finally giving myself some grace to allow myself to enjoy parts of life again, something I feel as though I have to practise now, because it doesn't come easily. I remember the time I felt as though I would never stop crying, that the tears were an endless river. It was impossible to consider that as time passes us by, a smile may come easily again. Somehow though, any kind of happiness is still tinged with this feeling of guilt, and a dull but present pain. Will anything ever be unspoiled, untainted, and just unapologetically *happy* again? Talking to new people where for just a moment I fooled them into thinking I was this free, whole and confident woman, not revealing my true identity, was a breath of fresh Welsh air! On this long weekend away, I could leave some of my grief unpacked back at the holiday home, and give myself a break.

On the sunniest day, we climbed a mountain. It was so picturesque, as we reached the peak and set up a resting spot to snack and gaze out at what was below us. Blue skies, clouds, the ocean and so much green. I watched as people were climbing. Men, women, families with eager kids and children of the fur kind, all striving and searching for the top of this mountain, and their daily dose of nature's finest endorphins. And I wondered to myself, what is their story? Who are these people, and what hardships are they trying to run, or climb from?

Is there another loss parent out there?

OLIVIA-GRACE
We finished...

I work with some amazing people. I have been so lucky to have had such constant support from people who were once strangers, and who since bonding over uniforms and coffee have become family. A friend at work, Sara, suggested we run. Run for you. There was a local event that we could be a part of, to raise money and awareness for a charity of my choosing. When she asked if we could run for you and raise money for a charity dedicated to HIE support and awareness, I think I jumped on her and hugged her so tight, I spilled her coffee! Someone, other than your immediate family, or me, wanted to do something for you. She acknowledged you, and your life, and wasn't afraid to bring up the topic of your brain damage with me, like so many others are. People must think I should come with a trigger warning, and they dare not breathe the words "brain damage" in my presence, in fear of causing an emotional breakdown. But it's the truth of what happened, and I want people to understand and respect our reality, however sad it may be. So, when Sara had this brilliant idea, she achieved so much more than just raising money in your name. She gave me a gift too, and I don't think she will ever know how much that meant to me. People say your name with such caution, or even avoid bringing you up in general conversation, like somehow they are going to upset me, and God forbid I should cry! I want them to know they aren't upsetting me. Quite the opposite. They are giving me the gift of remembrance, and that brings me comfort and faith.

I think when you lose someone so precious, it becomes instinct to want to do anything to protect their memory. To throw yourself into charity events, volunteer work, anything that means I can say your name and tell your story. I believe it's a welcomed and healthy distraction, and after all it's a personal choice to keep you present to me. I am not afraid to keep moving forward, but I will not move forward without you. I have been supported by friends and encouraged to do this, and for that I am grateful. I suppose us loss mamas just have to do whatever we need to do to get by. Some get tribute tattoos, some organise fundraisers, others get lost bingeing on junk food and chardonnay, and some run. Depending on the day, the mood, the weather… I do all of it! I try so hard to listen to my heart and do what is right for me in that moment. Doesn't stop the doubts that come, though. Should I have tried harder that day? Pushed myself to be a little more "okay"? Did I laugh a little too much? Should I have dipped these fleeting moments of happiness and light into a dusting of sadness and despair? Should I have been more sensitive when listening to the woman across from me complain about how exhausting and hard work her kids are? *They're alive, lady, complain to someone else please. Complain to a mama of the living, because just like you can't help me, I can't help you.* Am I stuck in my grief, afraid that living means losing more of you along the way? Crossing a finish line feels amazing, but some days, simply taking a shower is a massive accomplishment too. It took a while, but eventually I learnt that my achievements are immeasurable based on what other people think. How can someone possibly judge my choices and progress on this grief journey when they are just so fortunate to not even understand the daily challenges I face, living life as a mama to the dead? That on those bad days, getting out of bed takes more effort and energy than finishing a marathon.

My work buddy did a fantastic job at organising the whole thing. She took charge, and I agreed that I would simply show up on the day wearing my leggings and running shoes! In an effort to give it my all for you, I started training for the six-mile race in the bitterly cold weather of October. Turns out it was a welcome distraction to the normalcy of my new life, on just getting through each day, one way or another. Cliché I suppose, but it's a healthy habit and outlet I probably should have taken up sooner. Self-care while grieving requires an extreme amount of energy though, but as time continues to pass, I am finding that my own health, mental and physical, is creeping up the priority list. I am trying to do better all round. Trainers tied and headphones on, non-traditional but gentle running music playing through my earphones, I allow myself to get lost on my concrete track. I get lost in a place with just me and you. I let myself daydream about miracles, and the impossible. Protected time to live in a world of fantasy, and I enjoy it. I stop noticing the steps I have done, or how fast my heart is beating, and I just dream. Dream of what life could have been like. What would you have looked like? Whose hair or eye colour would you have, and what your smile would say to me? Denial again, perhaps, that I so openly and voluntarily choose to let myself visit a place I will never know. Knowing I'm opening the door wide open again to pain and heartache as I finally stop to breathe and remember that I am so far from the place I had just been visiting, so happy there, not wanting to leave. I do this two, or three times a week now. We go on a mummy and daughter running date. And I really do enjoy it.

I could not believe what Sara achieved. Over 20 of us ran that day. And we each wore a blue shirt with your name on the back, supplied by the charity we were supporting. We raised over £2000 for this UK-based charity. A wonderful and sensitive group of people that supports the families and those affected by HIE. It was a cold autumn day, but the sky was clear, and the sun shone so bright. There was a special feeling lingering in the crisp air. My hips hurt, I puffed and panted, and my cheeks glowed a burning glistening red; I am not an attractive runner. But with every step, I felt incredibly proud. I am proud of myself for being a woman so in pain, so traumatised and scarred, but a woman who could find some inner strength to literally run, when some days I could barely stand. I was so proud that I was the mama of the little girl printed on a bunch of shirts, a bright blue and yellow colour to stand out amongst a crowd of runners. That everyone running behind one of us would wonder, who is Olivia-Grace? And I knew that I had made you. You were mine. Something wonderful and surprising happened that day; I crossed the finish line in under an hour, met with loud cheers and claps from our loyal friends and cheerleaders. Tears in my eyes, for an amazing reason. How do you keep doing it, little miss? How do you make me so strong and determined when you are not even here? It's proof that your spirit exists inside me. Proof that a little piece of you exists in all of us.

A letter from Leanne...

Olivia-Grace; My angel baby's angel friend...

I met your mummy the day our baby, Freddie, was born, 5 March 2019. I woke up in the early hours to my waters spontaneously erupting, soon followed by contractions. It was happening. This was baby number three for us, our first boy after two beautiful girls. He was so wanted, my first son, and we couldn't wait to meet him. As labour progressed, everything seemed to be going well and so I was allowed in the birthing pool. I had nothing to be worried about, as I focused on letting the water soothe my pain, and I counted down the contractions until Freddie would be here in our arms. Labour soon reached its peak, but unfortunately it had become clear that Freddie was stuck, and quickly things turned into something more dramatic. They searched for his heartbeat to make sure he was okay, but they could only find silence. Freddie was finally born, but in poor condition. Freddie, our brown-haired boy, had been born with the cord tangled and wrapped tightly around his beautiful body and neck. He was rushed out of the room to be resuscitated. We were in complete shock, as we were unaware of any complications.

This wasn't supposed to happen, after a seemingly normal delivery, and nothing made sense.

We learnt that baby Freddie had suffered HIE, which meant his brain had been starved of oxygen. It felt like an eternity until we were finally able to meet our handsome boy, who weighed an incredible 9lb, 14oz. I remember the feeling of seeing him for the first time. I remember not wanting to. I was so scared. I was so scared of falling in love, and then not being able to keep him. Our baby boy, so young and new, who should be suckling at my chest, filling my heart with joy, was now fighting for his life. We began the transfer to the NICU, emotions still blurry, in physical and emotional pain, where they would take care of Freddie.

And this is where we met you, Olivia-Grace. Just cots apart, both perfect babies fighting the same horrific battle. Our babies had brain damage. Being told that your baby has HIE and may not make it was the most terrifying and heartbreaking thing anyone could ever hear. How did it come to this? My pregnancy was textbook, and Freddie was so perfect, so why? Why had this happened? Why to us? A lifetime of "whys". Freddie's sisters came and met their little brother. They read, held his hands and kissed his sweet head. Close family came and we prayed a miracle would happen. We spent eight days, now the most precious eight days of our lives, with our handsome boy. But on the eighth day, while in Mummy and Daddy's arms, we held our baby boy close as he took his last breath. Our hearts were broken.

But in the eye of the storm, I found a forever friend to trek these grief waves with. I found someone who would become another loss mum. We didn't know that's what our fate would be as we chatted, bleary eyed and tired, in the coffee room and found solace in each other's common heartache. In our darkest of times, we felt comfort in knowing that we weren't alone, that all that we felt was normal and shared. Freddie was the most perfect baby boy we could have ever dreamt of. Just so perfect, and I am so thankful everyday that he was, and is, ours. Since losing Freddie our life has changed in so many ways. Our family continued to grow, as our home and hearts were filled with rainbows. A forever friend was made when I met your mummy. I know she will always be a phone call away, and will always be there for us, even if her own journey is sometimes too much to bear. I will always be so thankful to have met you, baby girl, and have your wonderful mummy in our lives. If there is one thing I can promise you, Olivia-Grace, it's that no matter where our grief takes us, I will always be there to help guide your mummy and bring her as much comfort as I can; to remind her she is not alone. I hope our babies are dancing together in the sky, forever watching over us. We will never forget you, Olivia-Grace. Our baby boy Freddie's angel friend.

Love Leanne

Olivia-Grace, the proudest of smiles as we crossed the finish line, all because of you

OLIVIA-GRACE
Some shocking news...

I have been waiting for something to arrive in the post.

And today, it came. A large white envelope, but I did not want to open it. It was from the hospital, and any news from the hospital, I've learnt, can never be good. After you passed away, a formal investigation took place. Protocol, apparently. They do that for dead babies. All this time I had been searching for an answer. I had wanted an answer. Needed one. For what?! Closure? Am I desperate to find out what went wrong so I can direct all this anger and hate towards someone, or something? Lately I've just been screaming off into the universe. Shouting, swearing, crying at no one, but hoping someone hears me. But now, as I look at this envelope, I don't want to read it. I can't bear to read of you and what we had gone through in such a clinical, almost non-human way. You aren't just some report a random person conducted because they were instructed to; you are my baby. I don't need to be reminded of the events of that day, let alone to see them typed in black and white.

So impersonal. However, not reading it, as it turns out, isn't an option. With all the right intentions of sparing my heart any more pain, I have to read it. And with every word, black and cold on the page, a cold and sharp blade is being driven through every cell in my body. It stings like a bitch.

Placental abruption. An obstetric emergency that requires immediate intervention. The organ that was your lifeline, dying itself and taking you with it. This explains a lot of how my labour went. So unbelievably painful, so quick… I guess it makes sense now. Hindsight is a bitch. They found an answer and now I'm angry that I ever wished to know. Why couldn't I let it go and just believe this all happened by sheer bad luck? The worst luck. One minute you were fine, and then you were not. But now I know. I truly did fail you. My body failed in doing what it was supposed to do. Natural, they say. Giving birth is natural, *trust your body, listen to your body*. What a waste of time those prenatal and birthing classes were. My body completely let you down, it was my fault, and I will never forgive myself. Flashing back to those hours leading up to your dramatic arrival; *they should have noticed something wasn't right*. I felt it; I knew it in those moments of intense contractions, never letting up and suffocating me with every push; *this is too fast*. Why didn't they see something was going so horribly wrong? Why did no one do anything? They shouldn't have trusted me to keep you safe.

I feel sick. As I read on, my mind trying to absorb the details of those moments that it has previously blocked out, I wonder how the hell any of us missed this emergency. How did I not know what my body was doing? Was I so naive...? *Was I so stupid...?* And then, a spotlight in my brain, the numb and safe blurring of those memories disappears, and I suddenly relive the very moments just before your birth, and I can't breathe. *I can't breathe, and this hurts so much, and this is too fast... please... help me.* I can feel the rough and bloodied hospital sheet under my legs, the stink of body fluids, heat and sweat filling my nose until I'm gasping, and the room I had been sitting in, reading this report, suddenly looks so different. The walls are not the same. I'm back in that room, where my baby girl was born. *Why don't they know what's happening to you, hidden inside me?*

I remember back, my blind trust put in everyone in that room, including myself; *we should have known.* They should have gotten you out sooner, but no one did; they could have helped you if you were on the outside, where there was oxygen in the air, but you stayed inside too long.

I don't think I've ever felt so many difficult emotions like this, all at once. Rage, guilt, despair, hate, desperation, regret, *pain... pain... pain...* It's all rolled up into one burning ball of fire deep within my soul... My poor, sweet baby girl. I am, and always will be, so sorry. I think I will hate myself for an eternity. It was my job to protect you, and I failed. It wasn't my fault, I was told. There wasn't anything I did to cause such a catastrophe within my body; the abruption in itself was just bad luck. The words fall on deaf ears and a broken heart.

What would life have looked like if they had done something in time to rescue you? Would you have come home? Would I know your face, healthy and thriving? Would I have seen your rosy pink lips turn into a smile for me? *This is too much...* The thing is, I feel so messed up writing this, even thinking it, as though this feeling I have is a huge betrayal of you, but I still respect all the staff involved in the delivery of you. For them, it was just another Tuesday on shift. Another day of delivering babies and being a part of the best day of these parents' lives. A wonderful job that brings so much joy. Most of the time. They are good people, and good at their job, but *that* day, *that* Tuesday, I think that none of us were good enough. I want to blame someone. I want someone to take all the fury I can throw at them, because just sitting with all this guilt and anger is eating me alive. Even though these feelings of hate are entirely directed at myself, I'm already so full, the excess just hovers around me, a black and pained aura. I don't want to only feel hate and resentment when I think of you, baby girl. I don't want that.

But hate won't bring you back. Hate won't change my reality. The feelings just sit there, little miss, pulsing and throbbing with an angry beat of their own heart. Reading this report, knowing this, does it change anything? You're still gone. But I know deep down what I have to do now. I'm trying so hard to raise awareness and educate, as though in some way I'm saving a little piece of you if someone else can avoid this nightmare. Being pregnant with you, despite being medical myself, I had never even considered the possibility that an abruption could have happened to me. Did I miss any warning signs? Should I have known more of what labour "should" have been like? A little bit of knowledge, they say, is a bad thing. But maybe a little bit of knowledge could have saved you. This is my duty now, to advocate for change and awareness, to better standards of practice, so to spare another mama this heartbreak; *let her bring her baby home, alive and in her arms...* The idea of another internal fight to process this new understanding of the ultimate failure though; more reliving, more conflict adding layers to my grief… I'm just so tired. I've been in a war this whole time, I'm bleeding and broken, and now I have to start another fight to come to terms with exactly what happened and what went wrong. But I simply can't shut this envelope away, pretending it wasn't there, like I had initially planned. I'm sighing, knowing now that plans never bloody go to plan. I can't unknow what I know. To do that would be pretending that you were never here. That your struggles, and courage, and fight to live, were just another whistle in the wind. Here for just a moment and gone forever. I won't let that be, little miss. I'll fight for you, always. The bond we have, the love I feel for you, is stronger than death, and it lives on. And so, I will fight…

A letter from Uncle James...

Olivia-Grace; From my heart to yours...

When life is taken away, what would life be without death? Death is because there has been a life.

In that piece of heaven, beyond the rainbow bridge, a place to which I find myself wishing to retreat, to find sanctuary.

Life is but a journey, full of ups and downs, a rocky road of joy and pain.

From your eyes glistening like the night sky, we look to the stars, safe in the knowledge that you are shining bright.

From every little delicate white feather that falls, to the bed of the beautiful spring daffodils that bloom,

Every year,

Every month,

Every hour,

Every minute of the day... you give us those signs.

This may seem slightly disoriented, but it is from my heart. A heart that has felt its own eternal pain. A heart that was weak and broken, but you brought warmth and tenderness back into it, and I am truly thankful for that. While writing this, I was thinking of all the memories and mischief we would have gotten into, and I smile, a sad and longing smile.

Our little miss, it is time to say goodnight, sleep tight, and don't let the cradle bugs bite.

All my love, Uncle James

Olivia-Grace, a mother's kiss placed tenderly
on your cheek

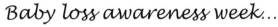

Baby loss awareness week...

That's right. There is a week to raise awareness and offer support to those affected by baby loss. I never knew. Why would I? Oh, how can I go back to a time where I didn't know this even existed? It makes me so angry, to my very core. How can we live in a world so unjust and cruel that we even need this carved-out week of time to raise awareness and attempt to make the world understand the unimaginable? No one, just no one, should suffer this kind of fate. But it happens, mostly with no questions answered or any kind of reasoning, and now I am a part of this special and sacred loss community. I am a permanent resident in a village of the taboo and unspoken, late-night insomnia-induced chats in the online forums and support groups. A village so surprisingly vast, with the wounded voices and shattered lives, who ask that same question every day. *Why me?* Why do *I* have to live this life? I weep to myself as I connect with other loss mums, and our lives, though oceans apart, blend together and we share each other's anguish. *Does it ever get easier?* The support and solace I have found among these ladies is overwhelming. I was so afraid to step into their world and introduce myself and you, maybe because it was another blow of reality and acceptance. You can't join one of these groups unless you have lost a baby. Rule number one. Babies born before they were ready, some born sleeping, the agony of the incurable, sweet babies who went to bed one night only to never wake, and others just like you, Olivia-Grace. Where these women's lives have been consumed by feeding tubes, therapies, and medication for their HIE warriors, and endless prayers and deals made with God, to just let them live. Tragically though, they have ended up where I am.

This week, everywhere I look I see pink and blue. I see candles and flowers, I see tributes. Buildings are illuminated in remembrance, and the morning news tells yet another harrowing story. Getting the tender and heartbreaking message out there that families really do have to live without their babies. They really do make coffins *that* small. I watch as a mother tells her child's story of sudden infant death syndrome, choking back tears, so that others may learn something, and another small and yet wonderful change to the world has been made. *You are so brave, Mama. We are here with you, and your baby. Thank you.* I read people's stories on social media, my group page flooded with women reaching out, and for that moment my heart connects so psychically with another loss mama and her angel baby. I hug them, I cry for them, and I cry for myself. It's as though we are all floating, somewhere above Earth but not quite to where our babies rest and play, holding each other's hand. We are the loss mamas, and we are very much here, living in a protected place you cannot come and visit. Hear us, and hear our babies' names.

My Ocean

I'm 29, and on a romantic holiday, bathing in California sunshine and turquoise seas,

I'm in love.

I'm 29 and on a long-haul flight back home, turbulence, jet lag, but smiling.

I'm 29 and going on... five weeks pregnant!

And glowing, and sick, and floating.

There's someone in the mirror as I get ready for work.

I think I recognize her but she doesn't quite look the same; hello, me...

She's a butterfly,

Almost...

I'm 29 and going on,

20 weeks and you're a girl!

And my world is pink, and swirly and twirly,

And kicks and wriggles, And so much pink.

I'm 29 and going on...

This is too fast.

This hurts too much.

What's happening, and why are you doing that to her, and why isn't she crying?

I'm 29 and going on...

A woman who just became a mother, but still isn't holding her baby,

It's...

I can't breathe,

You can't breathe,

There's not enough oxygen, and I need my own mother.

It's I can't save her, and you can't save me,

It's...

29 years old, and my baby died.

"Oh, I'm so sorry",

29 years old, my baby died.

"I hope you're doing okay".

29, my baby is dead.

29, I think?

And now there is a stranger looking back me,

No wings,

No beautiful explosion of colour,

She's dark, and old, And I'm scared.

"I hope you're doing okay...?"

And our eyes meet and I only see the reflection of my broken shell,

My eyes no longer blue but more grey, like ash, and burnt.

And I'm so grateful at times you don't know this pain,

I'm so grateful that all you have is pity in your eyes instead of true companionship,

I'm so grateful that your mini never turned into a memory, for this boat I'm drowning in is a loss mama's lonely voyage.

It's so lonely that at other times I wish you understood.

I wish you knew what this pain is.

I wish you knew what witnessing your lifelong dream's first breath is like, turned into their last as your heart continues to beat, while stopping at the same time.

I wish your...

Does that make me a monster?

Does that make me awful?

And cruel, and cold and unforgiving…?

Does that make me the very thing that took my baby girl away from me?

Does that make me brain damage?

Terminal.

Catastrophic.

When I wish you were in the same boat as me,

When I wish I wasn't the only mama to feel this,

When I wish for things I wouldn't wish on my worst enemy,

Somehow an angel's hand reaches down and touches my fragile heart.

And I promise…

As you're climbing onto this boat I am in,

The one I long to not be alone in,

As you pull your exhausted, wet and aching body up and I grab your hand, I promise.

I promise.

I promise I will let go…

*I'll let you go back into your ocean that isn't crashing
waves.*

*It isn't thunderstorms and lightning and black depths
swallowing you whole.*

It's calm.

It's soft.

It's crystal blue.

It's pink.

It's two pink lines, and "I'm going to be a mother!"

It's no fear, or guilt, or worry.

It's gentle, exciting and naive.

*It's lullabies instead of funeral processions and poems,
it's...*

*That's all I remember of an ocean I swam in a long time
ago.*

*An ocean I visited as a tourist; my time was up and I could
not stay.*

*Because my ocean continues to thrash my broken body
and soul...*

It tears me further and further from your ocean and all I want to do is jump ship.

But my baby, my little miss... She is my ship.

And my love for her is... my ocean.

OLIVIA-GRACE
"Coping" at Christmas...

I was fully prepared for the festive weeks to be torture. Or at least I thought I was prepared. It's my first Christmas as a mother, without my baby, so it was never going to be easy, was it? But it was harder than that. Christmas cheer, bright lights, my first Christmas onesies, steaming mulled wine and giggles among friends. And I hate all of it. Is there any advice appropriate to give a loss mum to help deal with the anger, pain, jealousy, longing and wishing they feel? Of course not. Holidays that simply ooze "family" and "picture perfect" are the worst. So, I open my heart to the crashing waves once again. I let them come in and drown me, and I close my eyes tight and ask you to stay with me. Keep me safe until the tide inevitably goes out and the crystal ocean that has drained my soul calms. I'm left with only fantasies now on how the day would have been, and I let myself daydream until I almost believe it. But as I sit out in the bitter cold of Christmas morning sipping on strong coffee, surrounded by the quiet joy of the holidays, if at all possible, I miss you even more.

I did have one little present early that morning, gifted to me, for you, by a dear friend. I opened it cautiously, and alone. How unbelievably thoughtful this gift was. A small and delicately carved wooden music box, varnished in love, as it played a song I haven't listened to in such a long time. Another one of your songs; our shower song, my favourite Disney song, and the song played at your funeral. "Colours of the Wind". Everything around me sat so still and paused, as we listened to this beautiful tune. My eyes cried a silent waterfall, with gratitude and love. This is our first proper occasion where you should have been passed around the room to every member of your family for cuddles, like the most precious gift that you are. There is no present on this Earth that can give me the same feeling as I got when looking into your eyes. Materialistic gifts mean nothing to me. And so, I keep myself busy cooking, playing with your fur sister and hosting to the best of my ability. Until finally, come the early evening and I'm worn out, the tears return. *It's not fair. This isn't how it was supposed to be, and I hate it. I don't want to do this, feel this, or live this anymore.*

I should have bought you a gift, so I could kid myself for just a minute as I wrapped it in Christmas paper, that you would be here to open it. I should have hung a stocking for you. I should have done something, and I failed. I'm so sorry. I just couldn't do it. How do you spoil an angel baby at Christmas? The thing is, I'm doing all that I know to do, right now. I suppose with time I will know better, and so I can do better. I will understand my needs around the special occasions, and what brings me comfort and a sliver of peace. I feel as though I let you down this Christmas, and I'm being hard on myself, but now I know. I need you here with me, somehow, to celebrate the wintry magical time that people love so much. So I decided, from this year on, I *will* hang a stocking; a festive one decorated with silver snowflakes, with your name carefully stitched. And I will write a note to you; a message of love, or a poem, and place it inside. It will be our little secret, between you, myself and Santa, and every year I will add another note. That will be our Christmas tradition; how does that sound, Olivia-Grace?

This time last year my belly was growing; you were doing somersaults to remind me of how big you were getting, and I was counting down the weeks until you stopped being a mystery love and best friend, and became so "real". It hurts to look at photos from a year ago. It hurts that I have to avoid the baby aisles in the store to save myself an ounce of pain, when this time last year I would have been racing to that very section. I could never have bought you enough. Everything I had, everything I was, was yours. Everything I am is still yours. It all makes ending this year and stepping (or being dragged?) into the new year so conflicting, my mind feels in a tug of war. This year has been the hardest, cruellest and most challenging year I could ever have imagined. But that being said, I never knew that I would feel the love that I felt. This year, 2019, will always be the best year yet, because I became a mother. A mother to a beautiful, strong, incredible baby girl. My baby, you made my own mother a grandmother for the first time. My brother an uncle. My best friends family-by-bond. And I have achieved some wonderful things. So, I suppose, thank you, 2019. Thank you for showing me unconditional love, purpose, and defiance. Thank you for reminding me of what I deserve, and that I am, and will continue to be, a damn good mother. But... I am glad you are over. Olivia-Grace, my gift to you is a poem… I hope that there is beauty within the words that reflect the beauty in your face.

A Christmas Wish

This mama sat quietly, in the armchair in the lounge,

The tree was well dressed and dazzling,

But she gazed at the gift-less space on the ground.

You see it's been a little while,

But the empty ache in my heart is still there,

And it's especially real at Christmas time,

Where the space where your gifts should be, lay bare.

I recalled my Christmas list, not more than a couple of asks,

Surely for someone so enchanted and magical,

These are easy, simple tasks.

So, I am asking, Santa, I'm begging and pleading,

To send a Christmas gift, that I have so badly been needing.

A gift that isn't wrapped in a bow, it doesn't cost a dime,

You see I long for my little miss,

That sweet baby of mine.

As the night drew darker, and the stars shone so bright,

It was time to rest my body and heart,

And so, I closed my eyes tight.

Then sometime later someone marvellous appeared,

*Nicholas himself, holding my Christmas list. "I'm so sorry
I can't give you what you want, that is just what I feared."*

With a sad and heavy heart, he thought long with intent,

This Christmas wish he could not fulfil,

He's seen so many times from Christmas lists sent.

*He knew he must do something, for the women who feel so
much,*

But what, he thought, could I send these mamas,

What gift from their babies' touch?

*And just like that he remembered the beauty of an angel's
wing,*

*And so gently and sweetly in my sleeping ear, he began to
sing.*

My dearest mama, my gift to you,

Look out for a feather, you'll know what to do.

So precious and white, perfect and pure,

Just like our angel baby, that's for sure.

I know it's a small gesture, I wish I could give you more,

I wish I could show you how content your baby is, now they've passed through Heaven's door.

But please take this small reminder, my little gift to you,

Let it fill your heart with warmth and love,

Promise you'll keep doing what you can do.

There's no strength like the mama of an angel, and some days seem long and so hard,

Especially at Christmas time when there is something special in the air,

Being strong simply feels like a façade.

But keep your eyes open, Mama,

There's a gift sent from up above.

It's a sign for you, you're doing amazing,

And it's sent from your baby, with love.

OLIVIA-GRACE

The clock strikes 12...

𝓗appy new year, little miss. We are officially starting 2020. I can't really work out how that makes me feel, knowing your birthday and angel-versary no longer match the year I'm writing down so frequently at work. I don't think I'm ready, as the numbers change on my calendar; you feel both further away from me, yet still ever so present. I know I can't stay in this crazy year though. I can't stop the world from dancing around the sun, as our burning star rises and sets every day, so do I.

I am living, and I'm doing relatively well. I've moved into a new house with someone special, and each room brings the excitement of a blank wall, that with some DIY and the interior design skills of your mother are slowly turning into a mosaic of your pictures and memory. I have survived my first December without you here, though at times I felt like I would collapse from lack of air under the waves of my grief tsunami. The intensity of my pain is still so strong, that in those moments, hours, and days of grieving, I feel as though I'm living in a time when I had only just lost you. I took refuge in my safe spaces, around my safe people. I drank too much red wine on the cold wintry evenings, in an attempt to shut out my agony. I went to sleep crying a river onto your urn which was cuddled up in my desperate arms, and I criticised myself much more than I should have. *I thought I was doing better.*

I am doing better, Olivia-Grace, and I am allowed to have huge feelings for the huge amount of love I have for you. I have no idea what this year will hold, but it was a surprising feeling when I woke up on the first day of the year with a quiet sense of optimism, my eyes looking forward, and hangover-free! I was expecting to feel like shit, mentally and physically. But I do notice there is a change in the wind that brings an air of anxiety. The universe has planted a timer, soul deep, as I know we are now counting down to February. To your birthday. The shifts in my moods are subtle to everyone else, but I can feel it. I'm on edge more, with a little less patience, and I'm scared. I know the anniversary of the day you made me a mama will be so hard, and my heart is ready and accepting to feel it all, but knowing that pain and all the loss feelings are waiting for me as the timer counts down is scary. With the addition of your pink blanket in my bed for extra comfort and encouragement, I hug you tight. I hug your teddy, your blanket, and I get lost staring at your photo. I may be scared, Olivia-Grace, but that doesn't mean I can't get through it.

"I used to build dreams about you." F. Scott Fitzgerald

Happy Birthday...

I'm a little late writing this for you, baby girl. I'm afraid we've even gone into a new month. The house is still decorated with daffs, though, and the sweet smell of spring wakes me up every morning. I tried a few times to write, my hands hovering over the keyboard, but I couldn't do it. Writing this journal to you has been so helpful to me, an outlet for my emotions, but reading this sad story and seeing it in black and white, sometimes what I want to say just doesn't type straight away. Some days I manage a few words to you; others my voice is lost, and I simply drift through the day. I'm sorry we had to wait, but there are things I need to say to you, and my heart has to be ready to say them. Forgive me. But, a little while on, I now sit and stare at my computer screen, anxious to begin writing, but I will be brave. I know exactly why this chapter is so hard. I know the sooner I start this chapter, the sooner I will finish, and that is scary because this is in fact my last entry into our journal. It is far from the end of our journey together though, little miss. I promised to write this first year. I promised to write and tell your story, the raw, painful, and beautiful truth of it all. And that is what I have done, to the best of my ability. But, my sweet little miss, your first birthday has finally come around. Happy Heavenly Birthday to you. One whole year since you blessed this Earth. Since you blessed my world and changed everything I once knew. I can't believe a whole year has passed. I sit here and wonder how I managed it. How did I possibly survive? After a year I'm pretty sure I am still winging it, playing each hour, each mood, each occasion by ear, dancing around the fragility of life. But saying that, even when the days seemed dark and endless, and those days came in abundance let me tell you, I always found a way to carry on, because the motivation was you.

The pain is still there, it still hurts in a very real and physical way, and the loneliness can be so loud and so consuming. I'm almost sure it will never go away completely, and so I continue to make peace with those agonising emotions and accept that, in some way, they are here for the long run. Remembering one year ago, frantic waves of terror, fear and agony swept over my body, until at 11:24 a.m. there you were, laid on my chest. But I could not look at you. I didn't hear you cry; I never heard you cry.

I could never forget that feeling, or what I saw when I first met you. Nothing could have ever prepared me. You were so pure and innocent, surrounded by all the clinical interventions that tainted everything that meant to be a baby. Everything had happened so fast, and I had no idea that this was simply the beginning of our fight and our story together. They told me you might not make the transfer to the NICU. Then they told me you might not make the night. But you did make it. You kept "making it" for over five weeks, and I will be forever grateful and in awe of you. That delicate little baby of mine turned out to be a badass wonder woman; how proud am I?! The tears start their escape down my face, and there is just no stopping them. I am sorry though; I remember promising you that on your birthday I would not feel sad. That this day is such a special one. But of course, our emotions don't deal the way we tell them to.

After I caught some breath back, I sat with an early morning coffee, and feeling brave, I watched your videos and got lost in that world I once lived in. The sounds of the machines, the exhaustion, fear, and love painted on my face, and your tiny body, half masked by wires and pipes. I scrolled straight to my favourite, to bless my ears once again, and I closed my eyes and listened to how your perfect

157

body jumped and danced with hiccups. I watched it over and over, until I could no longer see the screen through the fog and burning smoke that were my tears. I'm taken back to that room, those sounds, those smells. Your smell. For a second, as I breathed you in, I felt whole again; I felt as though you were with me. How can I not cry, little miss? When there are simply no words, you cry. I sat, and I cried, and I remembered. I played one of your songs over and over that normally I am too afraid to listen to, and I sang to you. "Colours of the Wind". I don't sing anymore, baby; I used to love to sing to you, especially in the shower as we lathered up and danced in the steam. You always kicked so hard then, but I've lost my voice. Will I ever sing again?

I didn't know how I wanted to spend this day. It didn't feel right, getting you a cake with a single, lonely candle. An incredible milestone, the number one, which we couldn't enjoy together. I don't take joy in the things we do to celebrate anymore. Cake, balloons, presents. I just don't seem to care for it. Your life of course is a celebration, but how can I blow that candle out for you, making a wish on your behalf that can never come true? I had to follow my feelings on this one and just do what felt right. Seems so disappointing now I look back, but what felt right was simply a walk with Naki and to sit on a bench hidden among the budding trees with a bunch of flowers and just be. I'm not sure how long I sat there, and I hope you sat with me. But the walk back home seemed further away than before, my body fatigued, eyes swollen, and my emotions drained. Later that day though, I had an unexpected courtesy message from a best friend to say that there was something waiting for me at my back door. My friends had given me space that day, allowing me to reach out when I was ready, but this present couldn't wait any longer. They wanted to wish you a happy birthday, little miss. A huge rectangle parcel in brown paper, and inside, a stunning piece of art. An image of the night sky, at the exact time, date, and location of your arrival. *Olivia-Grace, you were made of stardust, light and wonder, and we will always love you.* Words failed me when I tried to tell them how thankful I was, but they knew. It was such a heartfelt, appreciated gift that ended that special day with more tears, but also a smile.

Reflecting over this last year is so tremendously overwhelming. So much has happened, so much has changed. Has anything stayed the same, when I am no longer the same person? The depths of my world have shifted so much; people who have come and gone, the

159

goals, hopes and dreams I have had and lost. Love and laughter don't look the same as they used to, and they come from different places, but I'm embracing that, and I am so grateful that I have an army to carry me on the days when I am simply too weak. But I am hopeful, little miss. I am hopeful because I found out not that long ago that I am expecting a baby. A rainbow baby, some would say. A baby that comes after the loss of another. It signifies the end of a storm, the hope and peace once the rain has stopped pouring, and the wind is no longer howling.

I don't think that is quite true though. I see this gift more as streaks of bright colour and strength that cut through the downpour, raindrops splashed all over to shine a little more fluorescent. But the storm is still most definitely there.

I noticed one day that the sun set a little differently and shone new shades of yellow and orange. The wind felt new to me as the breeze twirled around my face; a gentler embrace than the bashing wind I was used to. And I realised that my eyes were looking forward instead of everywhere else that you may possibly be. It turns out that among all the twists and turns in life, the games we play and gambles we take, I found a surprising and comforting love which gave me faith in what the future may hold. I was so terrified of a life without that incredible love. Terrified of losing more of myself and what I could give to someone, because I had lost you. But what I was most afraid of was sharing a life with someone who never really knew who you were. Who had never seen your perfectly long feet and your rosy red pout. I was so afraid to move forward with someone new without being able to bring you with me. Maybe that made it easier to fall in love with someone who already meant so much to me. Who, over time gone by, had laid a foundation of trust and reliability, and was always there to carry some of my burden when I just couldn't manage on my own anymore.

You live so proudly in our home, your photos and tributes on display, and I know we are very much a blended family now. I truly believe this baby was chosen by you. Handpicked, precious and protected, by their big sister in heaven. I have to believe that, Olivia-Grace, I just have to.

I sit and talk to you, and think about you, and me, and this new baby, and tears stream down my face. A cocktail of tears, a sweet and bitter shot from every emotional bottle. I simply feel so much, it's impossible to write it all down. It doesn't change what you are to me though. You will always be my first baby. My beautiful baby girl. But to meet a new baby, knowing there is a part of you within their soul, a small reminder maybe, in the reflection of their eyes? My heart skips and swells to the idea of that. Somewhere deep within the fear, anticipation and guilt are glimmers of hope, excitement, and the promise of a new and growing love. A second chance perhaps. A second first-time mum.

I don't suppose people will understand what that even means. I'm already a mama, but I have no idea what to do. If my luck is different this time, I will bring my baby home. Swaddled and pink fleshed, breathing all on their own, and just living. How do I care for a healthy baby? How do I hold a baby free from a tangle of wires, tubes, and cannulas? With no nurse guiding me, supporting me, carefully and attentively watching my baby every minute of the day? How do I love this new baby as fiercely as I love you? I'm scared shitless. I have never parented a child free from life's greatest disasters. I will never know what it is, to just parent, as anything other than a loss mum. I promise though, for your special sibling, I will do my absolute best. I will learn how to wrap a tiny bum with no catheter in the way. I will learn how to breastfeed, taking cue from their natural ability to suckle. And I will learn how to love, without standing head on, staring death in its hideous face. I will learn how to mother without letting fear steal those amazing feelings. Should my body succeed this time, I promise, I will learn all of it.

Olivia-Grace, my sweet baby girl, I can promise you that I will never forget. It's impossible, when I am reminded of you all around me. I see you in all the faces of all the special people in my life. I smell your scent in the beauty of freshly cut flowers. I hear you when my heart- strings play along to your lullaby, and I feel you when I gaze up into the starry night sky, a mystical canvas telling a thousand stories, never to end. And so little miss, I'm going to tell you again, the words I wrote for the day we had to say our final goodbye to you. The day of the funeral – 17 April 2019. Even through all the soul-searching, the memories, the angry unanswerable questions to the universe, and all the love, these words are as true today as they were then...

I don't know what to say. I already know that there are no words that will ever explain the pain, anger, and confusion of this journey we were forced to go on.

I also know that there are no words that will ever do justice, when I try to explain my love for you.

For Daddy's love for you.

For all your family, and aunties', and uncles' love.

From the minute you were made, you were simply loved.

You are the strongest, bravest, prettiest baby I ever knew. You stunned and amazed me from day one.

I didn't know what to expect, or how I would feel as a mother.

Nothing could have prepared me for the feeling you gave me. You have taught me more about courage, pride, and unconditional love than I ever thought possible.

You fought so hard until the very end, because I know we both deserved to spend some precious time together, before you put on your angel wings.

Someone told me that these very special babies were never meant to leave our bodies. And that this way they are being returned to us, to be ours only, in our hearts for always.

My little miss, you are a piece of my heart. You are a piece of your daddy's heart, and we will forever love and adore you.

You may have only been on this Earth for a brief time, but you have left the largest footprints.

My little miss, you will not be defined as the baby who had brain damage. But as the beautiful baby who defied the odds, showed strength and stubbornness, who made us laugh after peeing in the doctor's hand, and who brightened the hearts of everyone who met you.

I wish I could have spent my life getting to know you, but you weren't destined for this world, Olivia-Grace.

We never gave up on you, baby girl. But we knew you deserved something so much better...

The sweetest melody plays in my ears, *how I wish you could rest your head close to my heart...*Olivia-Grace, I hope and long with all my being, that after this time, you too know, that I never gave up, and I will never give up. I could never have given up on you! That the way my life has been shaped, the change in my soul, is all because of you. On Earth or in Heaven, you were always my purpose. I hope I have made you proud, my sweet angel baby. And I am so unbelievably and eternally thankful that you chose me. Always and forever, I love you.

Olivia-Grace, life on the NICU was so hard, but I'd do it all again to be able to kiss you one last time

Milton Keynes UK
Ingram Content Group UK Ltd.
UKHW022034190923
428910UK00011B/105